FAKE NEWS IN CONTEXT

Fake News in Context defines fake news and sets it within a historical and international context. Helping readers to become more skilled at detecting misinformation, the book also demonstrates how such knowledge can be leveraged to facilitate more effective engagement in civic education.

Distinguishing between fake news and other forms of misinformation, the book explains the complete communication cycle of fake news: how and why it is created, disseminated and accessed. The book then explains the physical and psychological reasons why people believe fake news. Providing generic methods for identifying fake news, Farmer also explains the use of fact-checking tools and automated algorithms. The book then details how various literacies, including news, media, visual, information, digital and data, offer unique concepts and skills that can help interpret fake news. Arguing that individuals and groups can respond and counter fake news, which leads to civic engagement and digital citizenship, the book concludes by providing strategies for instruction and tips for collaborating with librarians.

Including a range of international examples, *Fake News in Context* will be of interest to teaching faculty and students of library and information science, communication studies, media studies, politics and journalism. Librarians and information professionals will also find a valuable resource in this book.

Lesley S. J. Farmer is Professor of Library Media at California State University Long Beach, USA, and the manager of the statewide ICT literacy project. She has authored over 30 books and edited three other volumes, mainly on library science.

FAKE NEWS IN CONTEXT

Lesley S. J. Farmer

Routledge
Taylor & Francis Group

LONDON AND NEW YORK

3776

BPJ3

First published 2021
by Routledge
2 Park Square, Milton Park, Abingdon, Oxon OX14 4RN

and by Routledge
52 Vanderbilt Avenue, New York, NY 10017

Routledge is an imprint of the Taylor & Francis Group, an informa business

British Library Cataloguing-in-Publication Data
A catalogue record for this book is available from the British Library

Library of Congress Cataloging-in-Publication Data
A catalog record has been requested for this book

ISBN: 978-0-367-40604-2 (hbk)
ISBN: 978-0-367-41680-5 (pbk)
ISBN: 978-0-367-81567-7 (ebk)

Typeset in Bembo
by Newgen Publishing UK

Visit the eResources: www.routledge.com/9780367416805

2|7|22

Dedicated to truthful and ethical professional news creators

CONTENTS

FIGURES

TABLES

1

INTRODUCTION

Byzantine historian Procopius did it, and Emperor Justinian suffered from it.

Reverend Henry Bate did it, and Queen Marie-Antionette suffered from it (Darnton, 2017).

American Revolutionary Samuel Adams did it, and President John Adams suffered from it.

We may never know who started #Pizzagate, but we know who suffered from it. These are all examples of fake news. Fake news about COVID-19 has also resulted in people drinking bleach, attacking Chinese people, or not taking the pandemic seriously – and dying.

At the time of writing, over seven million people have been diagnosed with COVID-19 and the U.S. Presidential election campaign is cresting. The "infodemic" of fake news is overwhelming the public. What should be paid attention to? Whom should we believe? How should we react? The fates of people and their governments hang in the balance.

As recent politics have made abundantly clear, news (i.e., a report of current events) might not be as true as it appears. At the same time, mass media play an increasingly significant role in today's society, as noted by Ireton and Posetti of UNESCO (2018). More than ever, people need to consciously and critically analyze and evaluate mass media messages, such as the news, and then decide how to respond. Of particular interest these days is fake news: **deliberate, publicly published fabrication/disinformation/hoax/lie purported to be real news**.

Several other kinds of information also mislead people (EAVI, 2017; Tandoc, Lim & Ling, 2018). Disinformation is a deliberate lie that has the intent to mislead its audience; fake news is a subset of disinformation, the difference being that disinformation does not have to be news. Misinformation, on the other hand, is incorrect information that is usually an honest mistake; it is not intended to fool anyone. Malinformation may be accurate, but its intent is to harm people. Bogus news – and bogus information – is fabricated; the motivation varies. News satire mocks news stories through humor and exaggeration. News parody mimics mass media, but incorporates non-factual information humorously to show the ridiculousness of the news. Both satire and parody depend on the audience to know the original news and compare it with the one-off joke. Propaganda is subjective information created by a political entity or other group to influence public attitudes. Sponsored content is information paid for by an entity, sometimes called native advertising, usually to support the sponsor's viewpoint. Partisan statements reflect one side of an issue, and are typically given by a political party member. Conspiracy theory is the belief that some event is the result of a covert influential group rather than some accepted reason. Pseudo-science is typically the misreading of actual science research or misinterpretation of data such as misleading statistical graphs.

As the above examples show, fake news is not new, and it's not going away. As long as people want to gain power or wealth, as long as people want to persuade others at any cost, fake news will continue. Fortunately, such people are a minority, even though their voices may seem to drown out other sounds. As more communication channels exist, and fake news can spread faster and wider than ever, it can seem that it constitutes a greater proportion of the news than in the past. However, the truth is that "real," accurate news has a larger first dissemination layer and lasts longer. There is hope. We should not become cynical, distrustful, withdrawn and desperate. We still have control over how we respond.

Thus, fake news is a wake-up call to the community at large to gain competency in critically analyzing and addressing fake news in particular and information overall. Indeed, the saying "Eternal vigilance is the price of liberty" applies to discerning and dealing with fake news. Fake news is everyone's responsibility. We need to keep current about the world around us as it affects us more than ever. We need to continue to learn about our world and be cognizant of its societal diversity, including points of view. We need to keep an open mindset, especially in these dynamic and changing times. We need to understand the varied forms of communicating and how each format shapes messages. We need to manage technology effectively and responsibly to access, utilize, create and communicate informed news as digital citizens. Civic engagement is a must in order for society to survive.

The more knowledgeable people are, the better equipped they are to deal with fake news. Learners need explicit instruction in critically analyzing news and other media messages, and they need to know how to participate effectively in public discourse to counter fake news and contribute competently in the civic arena. Fortunately, fake news also serves as an authentic context for formal and informal education, which can motivate learners' engagement. Because fake news involves a complex set of multi-disciplinary knowledge, skills, dispositions and actions, it serves as a relevant gateway to several literacies and life applications, thereby bridging academic and daily life.

In this respect, educators themselves also need instruction in these literacies so they have the competence to integrate them into the curriculum and link them to societal realities with the intent of giving learners authentic opportunities to practice those literacies responsibly and effectively. Fortunately, librarians are well positioned to leverage the hot topic of fake news to highlight the importance of information and media literacies, and incorporate them systematically into formal and informal education in collaboration with other educators and decision-makers.

As part of the news communication cycle, other stakeholders also need to step up their fake news game. News creators and disseminators need to follow professional and personal codes of ethics as they produce and disseminate accurate and insightful news. In the process, they need to show their transparency to their audiences and engage with them to build trust and collaboration. Decision-makers need to gather and analyze relevant news and other data effectively, listen to their constituents and provide opportunities for them to participate meaningfully, and seek the best outcomes for the public good. Families are children's first teachers so they need to model responsible behavior regarding fake news: accessing and managing the flood of news that they encounter, making informed decisions, teaching children positive values, and getting involved in their children's learning experiences. Participants at each point in the news cycle can be vigilant about fake news, as well as impacting the context of fake news. Such efforts ultimately benefit society at large.

In sum, identifying and addressing fake news is a critical life skill because it informs daily decisions and consequential actions within the context of daily life. Such efforts result in a virtuous information cycle as individuals become capable and contributing citizens, and ultimately impact the society in which they – and all of us – live.

What is the extent of fake news?

In 2013 the World Economic Forum called the viral spread of misleading information a "digital wildfire" global risk. By 2018 the University of Oxford found organized social media manipulation in 70 countries. According to a Pew Study (Mitchell et al., 2019), Americans see fake news as the most important issue in the country. During the latter part of the 2016 United States Presidential campaign, fake news was shared and commented more than real news, according to a 2016 Buzzfeed report. The same report found that over 100 pro-Trump fake websites originated in Macedonia alone. One Belgium company owns over 180 URLs dedicated to creating and disseminating fake news (Figueira & Oliveira, 2017). Rumors and disinformation constitute a major part of Asian social and political tensions, especially because of close networks and trust in like-minded associates (Yee, 2017). In Southeast Asia, this situation is exacerbated due to the uneven quality of journalism and lagging education standards that would otherwise enable people to discern fake news (Hutt, 2017). The extent of fake news and other disinformation was so great that the Oxford English Dictionary selected "post-truth" as the 2016 international word of the year (Berghel, 2017).

A 2016 Ipsos Poll found that 75 percent of people fall for fake news headlines. A 2016 Pew Research Center study revealed that almost a quarter of adults have shared a made-up news story, and two-thirds of adults say that fake news leads them to be confused about basic facts of current news, although more than three-quarters of adults feel at least somewhat confident about being able to recognize fake news.

Fake news has increased so much largely due to social media. Such Internet platforms are dynamic in nature, and facilitate attention-getting and sharing. Furthermore, fake news itself is a highly adaptive culture form that is hard to regulate or reform (Reilly, 2018). Even fake news regulation itself is problematic as it can devolve into censorship and limitations on freedom of speech. Who determines truth – and how? What are the criteria for fact-checking? What level of staffing, time and resources are needed to regulate fake news effectively? What accountability is linked to such regulation? These are knotty issues (Pamungkas & Putri, 2019). Fundamentally, it is everyone's duty to act knowledgably and responsibly in the creation, dissemination, access and use of news.

What are the consequences of fake news?

At the personal level, when people believe fake news, they are misinformed, and may make poor decisions. For example, parents have jeopardized their children's and other families' health because fake news (based on a misleading research study) claimed that vaccinations were harmful. Pizzagate, which resulted in threats and shootings, occurred because of individuals' responses to fake news about Hillary Clinton (Allcott & Gentzkow, 2017; Gyenes & Mina, 2018). Even if they don't commit dangerous acts based on fake news, when people don't know what to believe, they may become frustrated, polarized, more close-minded, confused, fearful, distrustful, cynical and withdrawn. Internationally, 39 percent of people surveyed by Reuters Institute in 2017 stated that they avoided news because it depressed them – or because they could not rely on the news to be true. None of this helps society.

Fake news has also tended to attack minority groups such as people of color or immigrants, the belief being that these groups threaten the existing "social order," meaning those in power (Grambo, 2019). Fake news is more persistent when it exploits tensions between groups, and reinforces pre-existing biases, resulting in increased polarization and off-screen violence. This kind of group libel or defamation is very hard to counteract if there is even a modicum of truth (such as the fact that Muslims were involved in the 9/11 attack). Furthermore, groups in power are less likely to be corrected by minority groups who don't have power, because those same minorities have less access to communication channels and may well be punished for what they say.

Fake news has also hurt mainstream media outlets. At the same time that fact-checking the news requires more time and staffing with the proliferation and sophistication of fake news, publishing deadlines have shortened and staffing has decreased. This situation is exacerbated with declining revenue as many advertisers have migrated to the timelier social media market. Furthermore, social media platforms facilitate the broadcasting of individual news items so that the link between editorial content and distribution has been largely severed. As early as

2009, researchers Gunter et al. found that Internet users preferred online news to offline news, and online news was trusted as much as offline news. As a result, mainstream media have less control and less power – and the proliferation of fake news has increased (Ireton & Posetti, 2018).

Even more substantial are the consequences of fake news on democratic processes. Russia is known throughout Europe as well as in the United States for spreading fake news and other disinformation to turn democracies against themselves by using hack attacks, terrorist online propaganda, fake news websites, and trolling (Benková, 2018). In Indonesia, protection rackets use fake news to aggravate section tensions and feelings of alienation (Azali, 2017).

Other consequences of fake news cross societal issues. Fake news has led to falling stock markets (Chen, Conroy & Rubin, 2015). Fake images in the news have primed racial stereotypes, with long-lasting effects such as anti-immigration actions and hate crimes (Messaris & Abraham, 2001). Fake news about vaccines has resulted in increasing cases of measles across the United States, conspiracy theory fake news about water fluoridation in New South Wales resulted in children being hospitalized for mass extractions because of tooth decay, and online fake news about health resulted in more Ebola-caused deaths in West Africa (Gyenes & Mina, 2018). These incidences are just the tip of the fake news consequence iceberg.

How can fake news be addressed?

Now is not the time to disengage, to withdraw from public discourse. It is not enough to delete fake news. Unhalted, fake news will continue unabated. Each stakeholder entity needs to address fake news: fake news creators and disseminators, government, educators and consumers. People need to become news and media literate. Those people who have accurate information need to step up and provide interventions and disseminate counter facts and stories. Enforceable policies and legislation need to be crafted, implemented and enforced by informed citizenry. These actions exemplify civic engagement: a hallmark of democracies. Indeed, fake news may be considered a clarion call to active citizenship.

How this book addresses fake news

This book explains the elements of fake news and its dissemination, and then provides resources and strategies that can help the educational community be savvy media consumers and producers – and be informed and civically engaged global citizens within the contexts of their own lives.

Chapter 2 briefly reviews the history of fake news, and details fake news' communication cycle.

Chapter 3 offers strategies for discerning fake news. News sources are compared in terms of their reliability and bias. Heuristics list criteria and general approaches for identifying fake news. Fact-checking tools use humans and algorithms to determine the accuracy of news. Collective intelligence leverages diverse expertise.

Chapter 4 asserts that stakeholders throughout the communication cycle need to take responsibility for addressing fake news. Each entity's role is then detailed.

Chapter 5 discusses several literacies that support the discernment of fake news, and suggests sample learning activities to help learners gain literacy skills. Significant literacies include news, visual, audio, digital, data, media and information.

Chapter 6 uses civic engagement as a framework to respond to fake news and practice digital citizenship.

Chapter 7 provides sample fake news curricula using a stand-alone and an integrated approach. The chapter also discusses instructional issues, and details the potential roles that librarians can play relative to curriculum, instruction and resources.

While high-profile fake news is associated with current events, the underlying elements of fake news are enduring, and need to be seriously considered. Fake news is everyone's responsibility. Eternal vigilance is the price of freedom, and civic engagement is a key factor in ensuring an informed citizenship. This book aims to help empower the reader to control fake news rather than to be controlled by it.

We can have the power. Use it for good.

References

Allcott, H., & Gentzkow, M. (2017). Social media and fake news in the 2016 election. *Journal of Economic Perspectives, 31*(2), 211–236.

Azali, K. (2017). Fake news and increased persecution in Indonesia. *ISEAS Yusof Ishak Institute, 61*, 1–10.

Benková, L. (2018). *The rise of Russian disinformation in Europe.* Vienna: Austria Institut fur Europa-und Sicherheiltspolitik.

Berghel, H. (2017). Lies, damn lies, and fake news. *Computer, 50*(2), 80–85.

Chen, Y., Conroy, N. J., & Rubin, V. L. (2015). Misleading online content: Recognizing clickbait as false news. In *Proceedings of the 2015 ACM on Workshop on Multimodal Deception Detection* (pp. 15–19). New York, NY: Association for Computing Machinery.

Darnton, R. (2017, February 13). The true history of fake news. *The New York Review of Books.* www.nybooks.com/daily/2017/02/13/the-true-history-of-fake-news/

European Association for Views Interests (EAVI). (2017). *Infographic: Beyond fake news.* Brussels, Belgium: EAVI.

Figueira, Á., & Oliveira, L. (2017). The current state of fake news: Challenges and opportunities. *Procedia Computer Science, 121*, 817–825.

Grambo, K. (2019). Fake news and racial, ethnic, and religious minorities: A precarious quest for truth. *Journal of Constitutional Law, 21*(5), 1299–1348.

Gunter, B., Campbell, V., Touri, M., & Gibson, R. (2009). Blogs, news and credibility. *Aslib Proceedings, 61*(2), 185–204.

Gyenes, N., & Mina, X. (2018). How misinfodemics spread disease. *Atlantic* (August 30). www.theatlantic.com/technology/archive/2018/08/how-misinfodemics-spread-disease/568921/

Hutt, D. (2017). Fake news, real danger in Southeast Asia. *Asia Times* (May 9), 9.

Ireton, C., & Posetti, J. (2018). *Journalism, "fake news" & disinformation.* Paris, France: UNESCO.

Messaris, P., & Abraham, L. (2001). The role of images in framing news stories. In *Framing public life* (pp. 231–242). New York, NY: Routledge.

Mitchell, A., Gottfried, J., Stocking, G., Walker, M., & Fedeli, S. (2019). *Many Americans say made-up news is a critical problem that needs to be fixed.* Washington, DC: Pew Research Center.

Pamungkas, R., & Putri, B. (2019). *Fake news in the mid-2010s: Emergence, implications, and the global enterprise.* Yogyakarta, Indonesia: Center for Digital Society.

Reilly, I. (2018). F for Fake: Propaganda! Hoaxing! Hacking! Partisanship! and Activism! in the fake news ecology. *The Journal of American Culture, 41*(2), 139–152.

Tandoc Jr, E. C., Lim, Z. W., & Ling, R. (2018). Defining "fake news": A typology of scholarly definitions. *Digital Journalism, 6*(2), 137–153.

Yee, A. (2017). Post-truth politics & fake news in Asia. *Global Asia, 12*(2), 66–71.

2

THE COMMUNICATION CONTEXT

Fake news is not a singular phenomenon. It reflects universal human emotions and action, and it exists within very nuanced settings and situations. In short, to understand fake news, one needs to explore its human creation and interaction.

A brief historical background

To understand fake news, it helps to have some background information about it. The term "fake news" may be relatively new, but the concept is old. In political circles, there is recorded evidence back to Octavian's propaganda against Mark Antony via coins etched with negative slogans (Posetti & Matthews, 2018). In Byzantine times, smear tactics were written against the Emperor Justinian. French canards date back to the 17th century with broadsides featuring the capture of monsters and later denigrating Marie-Antoinette as a political monster (Darnton, 2017). The burgeoning newspaper *The New York Sun* published the first large-scale news hoax about the discovery of life on the moon (Uberti, 2016). With each "new" mass media format – be it the printing press, radio, television or the Internet – has come fake news.

Current fake news has more potential influence than ever because technology facilitates the broad-based and speedy creation, global dissemination and access to fake news (Ireton & Posetti, 2018). Further validating fake news is the uncoupling of content and dissemination. Whereas newspapers and television, as examples, both produce and curate news to be broadcast as a "package" of information, algorithm-based social media pick and choose from a variety of news sources without a cohesive whole. The news reporter and editor have less control over their products once those products are disseminated. Furthermore, with the former media, one false story can impact the reputation of the entire media outlet, so the stakes for delivering accurate news are high in contrast to bite-size news snippets that can be disregarded as false without compromising social media as a whole.

Thus, while mainstream media outlets are making greater effort to suppress or delete fake news, controlling bot-based algorithms and viral sharing demands extensive staffing and time to fact-check the rampant disinformation. Even if such checks were possible, ethical questions about censorship and freedom of speech come into play (Jang & Kim, 2018). More fundamentally, who decides what is true? In any case, as fake news titillates the senses and emotions, and can be easily spread, the chances that fake news will disappear for future historians to analyze are slim (Rainie, Anderson & Albright, 2017).

The communication cycle of fake news

To understand how fake news works, one can contextualize it in terms of Schramm's 1948 communication model: from the internal idea to the way it is communicated and contextualized to issues of access, processing and resultant action. Basically, the sender (transmitter) externalizes an internal idea as a mediated message (e.g., an oral speech, a written essay, a photo selfie), which is transmitted through a medium (e.g., radio signal, television, Internet). The sender may have specific receivers in mind, or not. The receiver encounters the message, and may decide to engage with it: decoding it if possible, possibly understanding it, reacting to it, possibly acting on it, and possibly sending a message back to the sender. Both sender and receiver have a field of experience, which impacts the message, its understanding and its reaction. In addition, the transmission medium can experience interference and noise, such as environmental distractions, quality of the communications medium itself (e.g., static, rain-soaked paper, power outage). Each step along the way can alter the message or its reception.

Creating fake news

Who creates fake news? Anyone can; the process is easier than ever because the message can be created in so many formats. A lone individual, a private or public group, a government, even a cyborg or bot can create fake news.

Why create fake news? To assert power and influence, to gain attention, to have fun – or to make fun of others, to harm, and to make money. Historically, the most impactful fake news has tried to influence the masses. Some people like to make up fake news to get attention or a reaction, be it an April Fools' joke or a Halloween prank; even then, the consequences can be impactful, such as the unintended reaction to Orson Welles' radio show "War of the Worlds" (which did have a caveat about its fantastic basis at the beginning of the broadcast). More recently, Internet trolls have displayed serious asocial online behaviors that have embarrassed, offended and marred people's reputations, although such intent to harm also has a long history, sadly (Bradshaw & Howard, 2017). Fake news has also been created to make money: to sell more newspapers as witnessed in yellow journalism, to get people to buy a disreputable product such as swamp land or snake oil, and more recently to earn money from writing fabricated stories for websites sponsored by advertisements based on reader clicks (Shane, 2017). For instance, a sizable industry emerged in Macedonia during the 2016 United States Presidential election campaign, which combined all of these incentives to create fake news. Sadly, fake news has also been weaponized by governments to divert attention from their mishandling of crises such as the COVID-19 pandemic as a way to prevent domestic criticism or to undermine confidence in opposing groups such as scientists (Schulman & Siman-Tov, 2020).

Fake news is created in several kinds of contexts, such as politics, religion, business, science. The most obvious context is political, be it to elect, support or dismiss officials; influence political action (e.g. war, rationing, construction); influence legislation; or influence allocation of resources (Kriel, 2017; Pestalardo, 2006). As is well documented, Russia has spread fake news and disinformation in general via many languages through many media channels in order to turn open democracies against themselves (Benková, 2018). In South Africa, a powerful family hired a British public relations firm to write fake news against the president, and the ruling party used fake news as a rhetorical tool to attack journalists (Wasserman, 2017). In Southeast Asia, governments want to control social media outlets so they use fake news to intensify censorship of journalists (Hutt, 2017). South America has witnessed several years of fake news and other disinformation attacks by fake organizations who target government officials, lawyers and journalists; at the same time, news outlets are being constrained (Scott-Railton et al., 2015). It should be noted that political influence may also be expressed in the form of propaganda, a one-sided view of an issue similar to one side of a debate, but the information itself may be true unlike fake news that is patently false (Chomsky, 2002).

Religion is another fake news hot button issue, particularly because it is frequently central to one's self-identity or value system. For instance, in India fake news about religion has spread for years, even before the rise of the Internet, resulting in deaths and displacements of religious groups (Bhaskaran, Mishra & Nair, 2017). In China, a provincial association started rumors about a Christian sect, and the government took advantage of the fake news to create anti-cult propaganda (Folk, 2017). 9/11 flamed anti-Muslim fake news and subsequent immigration restrictions. Anti-Semitic fake news has occurred for millennia, resulting in diasporas and genocide.

Science has become a major target for fake news in recent years, from anti-vaccination efforts to denials of global warming. As factions become less tolerant of alterative scientific ideas and more polarized, they have created fake news to counter scientific findings (Lazer et al., 2018). Especially when people have limited access to scientific journals or are not science literate, they are more likely to believe pseudoscience claims (Peters et al., 2018). In tracing Tweets about COVID-19, Pulido et al. (2020) discovered that false information about the pandemic was tweeted more than science-based evidence, although scientific information was retweeted more, largely because the information provided more extensive treatment. In fact, Kucharski (2016) compared the spread of fake news to the spread of a disease, through social contact. He claimed that as those social contacts become more localized, the diversity of the circulating strains (of fake news) can increase. In some cases, science itself may be at fault. For instance, claims about drugs have not undergone rigorous testing, or the test results have been skewed to sell more products. Inaccurate science studies may be retracted, but news about the studies might have already spread widely. Furthermore, science news can be over-sensationalized or exaggerated by media outlets seeking a greater audience. For example, early news about COVID-19 both under- and over-estimated its extent, resulting in people either dismissing the virus or panicking (Ioannidis, 2020).

Another important aspect of fake news creation is advertising. In particular, government and political parties sometimes employ advertising entities to create fake news to support their agendas and discount opposing views. In analyzing advertisements that mention COVID-19, Mejova and Kalimeri (2020) found that advertisers leveraged the pandemic to attack politicians, promote businesses, and solicit money for different causes, including animal rights. At this point in time, public relations (PR) and marketing firms around the world establish fake accounts and disseminate fake news for the right news; similarly to military mercenaries they act as information (fake news) mercenaries (Silverman, Lytvynenko & Kung, 2020). In the last nine years, at least 27 online fake news operations have been at least partially attributed to PR and marketing firms, who have been motivated in part by financial incentives.

Disseminating fake news

Fake news as a message targets some kind of intended audience: the general public; groups of people such as religious members, political parties, ethnic groups, professions, social organizations and so on; governments; foreign entities; and individuals. Frequently the message is *about* specific populations (e.g., abortionists, Communists, women gamers), addressed to other people who might be able to influence those intended audiences. For instance, messages about recent immigrants might be targeted to a political party in the hope that the party can create legislation to depose those immigrants.

The message and the intended audience largely determine how fake news is spread. Generally, media outlets, including social media, disseminate fake news. The global reach of the Internet has been particularly effective for creating fake news in one country and disseminating it in another country (e.g., Cambridge Analytics) as well as spreading fake news that has international implications such as economic trends.

The Internet has significantly facilitated the speed and reach of news, including fake news. Within the Internet, social media has seen the greatest growth; as of 2017 social media is a source of news for two-thirds of Brazilians and almost half of Australians on a weekly basis; Germany has a much lower percentage, 29 percent, but other European countries range from a third to two-thirds of their populations using social media as a source of news at least once a week (Newman et al., 2017). Now more than ever, people are inundated with news. Yet they have no additional time to scroll through all the news to evaluate and select authoritative sources (Tandoc et al., 2018). Further exacerbating the issue, social media makes it all too easy to share news, be it accurate or not, and people are likely to believe what their friends say is true (Mukerjee, 2017). Within the first five hours of dissemination, fake news and other disinformation spreads differently from real news; it spreads faster, deeper and broader (Jang et al., 2018). A MIT report (Meyer, 2018) revealed that a false story reaches 1500 people six times quicker than a real story, on average. Early adopters repost fake news quickly through more informal channels. In contrast, mainstream media outlets have a large first dissemination layer and their news lasts longer (Zhao et al., 2018). As a result, fake news can spread faster than truth and reach up to ten times as many people as real news because of the content's novelty and emotional attraction (Vosoughi, Roy & Aral, 2018).

These trends seriously impact mainstream media outlets who hold to ethical standards of verifying information before publishing it; such responsible journalism takes time and staffing, which can be costly. The sad reality is that it takes much less effort and money to make up news than to seek and gain information, and then verify its accuracy. When time is of the essence and newsworthy items can become stale in a matter of hours, these added checks are sometimes shortcut, leaving those same media outlets vulnerable to fake news themselves and possibly tarnishing their own reputations. Furthermore, as media outlets incorporate social media into their portfolios of communication channels, they are pressured to conform to those looser social media norms (Cheruiyot, 2019). Adding to the problem, mainstream news outlets themselves sensationalize headings and photos to get more reader attention; as a result, consumers have an even more difficult time parsing real news from fake news.

In contrast, the short-term perspective of social media lowers the stakes of inaccurate news. Even viral fake news is likely to have a short life span. When fake news is "found out," the creators can justify their actions by proclaiming the protection of the first amendment: freedom of speech. Particularly since libel and slander of public figures are difficult to prosecute, unlike for private individuals, fake news creators usually have greater leeway to create misleading information and give questionable opinions. Such creators can also use the claim of parody and satire to cover possibly damaging statements (Kirtley, 2018).

Accessing fake news

Why do people access fake news – and pass it on? The reasons lie within the brain as well as within people's experiences and contexts. Engagement with fake news also reflects the nature of social beings.

People are most likely to encounter fake news through social media. While people trust newspapers more than social media, two-thirds of people access news via the latter (Martens et al., 2018). In Singapore and Malaysia, a quarter of the population use social media as their main source of information; a seventh of Americans and a twelfth of British people consider social media as their main news source (Yee, 2017). It should be noted that social media access depends on access to the Internet and on digital literacy. For instance, older people are more likely to get their news from television, the medium they grew up with, unlike the newer social media platforms (Diehl, Barnidge & Gil de Zúñiga, 2019). In contrast, young adults access news via multiple modes and multiple social sources, both via social media platforms and face-to-face human contact (Head et al., 2018). Indeed, the number one way of getting news for them is discussion with peers (93 percent), and within a week two-thirds of young adults receive news from five communication pathways (e.g., discussion, social media, online newspapers, news feeds and television).

Creators and disseminators of fake news make a conscious effort to get the consumers' attention so they will engage with, and believe, fake news. Clickbait uses prominent placement, bright colors, incongruent and arousing images, and bold text to draw the eye and encourage one to click on the fake news link. Linguistic techniques also grab consumers' attention and keep them involved through reading and sharing: these include active verbs, provocative adjectives, shocking numbers, celebrity names, innuendo, humor and suspenseful text (Bakir & McStay, 2018; Chen, Conroy & Rubin, 2015). In addition, tagging the web content can influence the likelihood of gaining attention (Baeza-Yates, 2018). For decades, advertisers have used consumer motivational research and other psychological techniques to attract and engage consumers. To keep the consumers' attention, fake news, similarly to advertisements, appeals to people's compelling needs: emotional security, love, reassurance of worth, ego gratification, sense of power, social roots, and immortality (Packard, 1957). In terms of the kind of news that people are most likely to click on, Tenenboim and Cohen (2015) found that people gravitated to crime, death, the curious and the sensational. Fundamentally, fake news typically uses emotionally-charged content and images to stimulate the consumer's empathy, bypassing reason.

The process of choosing which news to access largely depends on the consumer's interest; if it is outside their knowledge base or doesn't seem to be relevant to their daily life, they are more likely to ignore that news. Similarly, people are more likely to seek out news that confirms their current attitudes and beliefs (Flintham et al., 2018). Individual capital also impacts news choice; people with rich cultural experiences develop patterns of taste that lead to consuming "quality" news rather than "popular" news, in contrast to the behaviors of people with less cultural capital (Ohlsson, Lindell & Arkhede, 2016).

Especially when people feel overwhelmed by the amount of news, they tend to choose the most convenient source and depend on their friends' choices so they don't have to decide for themselves. In that respect, media "branding," such as a favorite television channel or magazine that curates and collates the news, is an appealing solution (D'Costa, 2016). Online algorithms leverage convenience in that they can track user online news choices to then boost the ranking of subsequent similar news, making it easier for the consumer to access news with the same bias.

Such algorithms are effective because they draw from user behaviors and are based on emotional needs to belong and seek public recognition (Hirdman, 2019). At the same time, such algorithms lead to a loss of diverse opinions, effectively creating a filter bubble (Pariser, 2011; Spohr, 2017). Such practices often escape the users' consciousness, so people might not consider the implications, which may lead to bad decisions (Reilly, 2018).

Processing fake news

How people internally process information reveals why they might believe fake news. Belief in fake news also draws upon biological reasons such as brain circuitry, as well as psychological aspects of cognitive and confirmation bias. As noted above, noticing fake news involves the senses first, then the emotions.

The medium itself impacts how fake news is processed. For instance, television seems more first-hand and authentic because of its visual reporting. Especially if its message is presented with cross-media accounts, consumers are likely to believe it (Toggle, 1998). People also tend to base their judgment on the source; that is, they generalize about the information presented by the media outlet rather than evaluate the variation in quality of each news item, or consider that the source might be just re-reporting news from another source, such as a news wire service (Flintham et al., 2018). On the positive side, in light of the range of news about COVID-19, Europeans are depending more on reputable mainstream news organizations and trusting more in science and health experts (Nielsen et al., 2020). On the other hand, recognizing this trusting behavior, fake news creators sometimes utilize website spoofing, whereby they create a fake website that visually resembles a legitimate website in order to fool the reader (Felten et al., 1997).

Next, is the brain stimulated by the content; is the news novel, understandable, interesting, relevant? If the news piques one's interest, that person is likely to engage with the news. A more difficult issue is whether to accept the news as fact, opinion or falsehood. News is not monolithic; some items are strictly factual, such as the date of an event or the final score of a game. Some articles have the intent of making sense of the news by explaining the context of the news or providing additional facts. Other news items are opinion pieces that analyze and assess the news; they are based on expert judgment but should not be taken as absolute fact (Kovach & Rosenstiel, 2010). Further blurring the validation picture, fake news writers usually incorporate enough truthful statements, especially at the beginning of the news item, to build a foundation of trust so that the later fake elements will also be believed. Similar to debate techniques, these writers cherry-pick those facts that support their side and omit conflicting facts. This process is called selective sharing, and is very effective because the source of the information can be dutifully cited and most people will not take the time to read that original source to uncover the whole story (Kahneman, 2011; O'Connor & Weatherall, 2019).

Another decision point concerns the alignment of the news to the consumer's point of view (Flintham et al., 2018). Everyone has a unique perspective and bias, based on experience, knowledge base, attitudes, values and personality. When news confirms one's biases, then it is more likely to be believed; when it contradicts one's biases, then it is more likely to be rejected. This phenomenon is called confirmation bias (Cook, 2017). The more that the news addresses a core value or sense of identity, or the more extreme one's beliefs, the more vulnerable the person and the more volatile the reaction either for or against that news (Kaufman, 2019). For instance, American political parties are influenced by political news; if the information aligns with their political beliefs, then that party's members are more likely to consider it factual, while if it conflicts with the party line then those same members will consider that news opinion rather than fact (Mitchell et al., 2018). Furthermore, when no prior stance has been established, the first news about a topic that a person chooses to read sets the baseline expectation, all other factors being equal. The second news item on the same topic, if it contradicts the initial story, is less likely to be believed, even if it is more factual. Since it takes more effort to seek different perspectives, it is likely that the person will respond to just confirming versions of that news, even if it is fake (Yagoda, 2018).

People with less cognitive ability or reasoning skill are more susceptible to fake news and more likely to share it. Moreover, when subsequently given the current news, they are likely to stick to their belief in the original fake news; the initial influence is not undone (De keersmaecker & Roets, 2017). In contrast, people with more analytical ability are more likely to discern fake news from real news, and are less likely to share news on social media. Similarly, people who are politically aware and digitally savvy are better able to distinguish between true and false news (Mitchell et al., 2019). In terms of exposure to news, people who are heavily exposed to fake news and little exposed to hard news are more likely to believe fake news in contrast to people who are exposed equally heavily to fake and hard news (Balmas, 2014).

Young people are also more vulnerable to fake news because they have more difficulty evaluating the credibility of news (McGrew et al., 2017). Thus, belief is more a question of susceptibility than motivated agendas (Pennycook & Rand, 2019). Young people are also significantly influenced by their peer social groups' recommendations, which largely stems from heavy social media use (Nee, 2019). On the other hand, young adults are likely to receive several sources of the same news event, so they can cross-reference the news and explore different treatments (Head et al., 2018). These phenomena occur in adulthood as well, and illustrate the sociological context of processing fake news. People tend to believe the links that their friends believe and share, which can shape people's collective memory when fake news is repeated. This action fosters social bonding and lowers a sense of uncertainty. Especially if those fake news links are introduced before individuals have a chance to discuss the verity of that content within the group, that fake news can strengthen group cohesion and distort their views of outsiders (Spinney, 2017). Similarly, culture biases share personal beliefs and cognitive biases, and impact people's acceptance of fake news in order to align themselves with their cultural group (Baeza-Yates, 2018). In either case, when opposing or corrected information is encountered afterwards, these groups tend to dismiss the newer challenging information, and tend to cling on to the initial fake news, in order to maintain their social currency (D'Costa, 2016). In that respect, receiving several versions and perspectives of the same news event within a tight timeframe helps to mitigate fake news impact (Head et al., 2018). When, instead, all the news received is similar, it results in a social echo chamber that reinforces the same ideology and omits alternative perspectives. Echo chambers make people more vulnerable to accepting rumors, especially if those people are segregated from other groups. Algorithms developed in the course of creating fake news leverage this behavior, tailoring the fake news message to groups rather than trying to personalize the message, which takes more effort (Menczer, 2016); the result is a type of cognitive mind control that creates a mental model that cannot be interpreted in different ways (Van Dijk, 2006). Algorithms and social bots can exploit popularity biases and repeatedly feed consumers fake news, thereby constructing filter bubbles that further cut out fact-checking corrections (Shao et al., 2017; Ciampaglia & Menczer, 2018).

Acting on fake news

Not only do some people believe fake news, but they pass it on. The Pew Research Center (Rainie, Anderson & Albright, 2017) found that almost a quarter of Americans have shared a fake news story, often because they have read only the headline. Twitter users are 70 percent more likely to retweet fake news than accurate news; they are more likely to spread fake news than even bots do (Meyer, 2018). Almost three-fifths of young adults share news at least weekly; almost a quarter of them share news daily, the main topics being politics, lifestyle and education (Head et al., 2018). Their motivation is largely to inform peers about something considered important to know, although they do not validate news for personal use to the degree they do for academic purposes. Gender also impacts sharing behaviors. Women use Facebook more than men, and they share more, but the content tends to focus on consumerism and relationships; men tend to talk more about politics and share with a smaller online network (Mellema, 2014). These online behaviors impact fake news access in that it fosters peer dependence and information echo chambers. In fact, Asmolov (2018) asserted that fake news might be said to be co-constructed by the audience in that they negotiate the meaning of fake news, and in restating it or sharing it, that fake news gains more currency.

Mainstream media outlets are also guilty of picking up, believing, and then publishing fake news as true. This action typically happens under very tight deadlines. Fake news creators can then cite that publication as a verification of their own fake content. By referring to that mainstream appearance as the original source, the fake news creator can pose as just a sharer. This process is called circular reporting, and is used to reinforce belief in fake news (Hurley & Smith, 2019).

Repeatedly encountering fake news can wear a person down. One solution is to limit the time spent reading and the sources being accessed. As a consequence, both fake and real news may be ignored, which makes one a less informed decision-maker (Graham, 2019). Alternatively, an overload of fake news may result in persons becoming cynical, doubting the veracity of all news, and alienated from civic engagement as a whole (Balmas, 2014).

Beyond polarizing thought or negatively impacting people's attitudes about certain groups, fake news can inspire people to act upon their emotions. The COVID-19 pandemic is a case study in unfortunate consequences. Based on fake news, people drank bleach, thinking it would prevent illness. In India, people boycotted stores out of fear that poultry carried the virus (Goel & Yadav, 2020). Fake news has incited violence such as harming Chinese and people of Chinese descent solely based on the fact that the virus started in China (Imhoff & Lamberty, 2020).

While many people feel that they can spot fake news and are not influenced by psychological ploys such as clickbait, they are in fact often fooled and sometimes exploited, particularly in terms of their biases. The good news is that when people are confronted with their biases, they become less biased – again on the unconscious level to a large degree (Nelson, 2013). More fundamentally, though, media literacy is necessary to discern and evaluate fake news.

References

Asmolov, G. (2018, September 18). The disconnective power of misinformation campaigns. *Journal of International Affairs*, *73*(1). https://jia.sipa.columbia.edu/disconnective-power-disinformation-campaigns

Baeza-Yates, R. (2018). Bias on the Web. *Communications of the ACM, 61*(6), 54–61.

Bakir, V., & McStay, A. (2018). Fake news and the economy of emotions: Problems, causes, solutions. *Digital Journalism, 6*(2), 154–175.

Balmas, M. (2014). When fake news becomes real: Combined exposure to multiple news sources and political attitudes of inefficacy, alienation, and cynicism. *Communication Research, 41*(3), 430–454.

Benková, L. (2018). *The rise of Russian disinformation in Europe.* Vienna: Austria Institut fur Europa-und Sicherheiltspolitik.

Bhaskaran, H., Mishra, H., & Nair, P. (2017). Contextualizing fake news in post-truth era: Journalism education in India. *Asia Pacific Media Educator, 27*(1), 41–50.

Bradshaw, S., & Howard, P. (2017). *Troops, trolls and troublemakers: A global inventory of organized social media manipulation.* Oxford, UK: University of Oxford.

Chen, Y., Conroy, N. J., & Rubin, V. L. (2015). Misleading online content: Recognizing clickbait as false news. In *Proceedings of the 2015 ACM on Workshop on Multimodal Deception Detection* (pp. 15–19). New York, NY: Association for Computing Machinery.

Cheruiyot, D. (2019). *Criticising journalism: Popular media criticism in the digital age.* Karlstads, Sweden: Karlstads Universitet.

Chomsky, N. (2002). *Media control: The spectacular achievements of propaganda* (Vol. 7). New York, NY: Seven Stories Press.

Ciampaglia, G., & Menczer, F. (2018, June 21). Biases make people vulnerable to misinformation spread by social media. *Scientific American.* https://theconversation.com/misinformation-and-biases-infect-social-media-both-intentionally-and-accidentally-97148

Cook, G. (2017, September 27). Understanding the influential mind. *Scientific American.* www.scientificamerican.com/article/understanding-the-influential-mind/

Darnton, R. (2017, February 13). The true history of fake news. *The New York Review of Books*. www.nybooks.com/daily/2017/02/13/the-true-history-of-fake-news/

Diehl, T., Barnidge, M., & Gil de Zúñiga, H. (2019). Multi-platform news use and political participation across age groups: Toward a valid metric of platform diversity and its effects. *Journalism & Mass Communication Quarterly, 96*(2), 428–451.

D'Costa, K. (2016, November 28). Understanding the social capital of fake news. *Scientific American.* https://blogs.scientificamerican.com/anthropology-in-practice/understanding-the-social-capital-of-fake-news/

De keersmaecker, J., & Roets, A. (2017). "Fake news": Incorrect, but hard to correct. The role of cognitive ability on the impact of false information on social impressions. *Intelligence, 65*, 107–110.

Felten, E., Balfanz, D., Dean, D., & Wallach, D. (1997). *Web spoofing: An Internet con game.* Princeton, NJ: Princeton University.

Flintham, M., Karner, C., Bachour, K., Creswick, H., Gupta, N., & Moran, S. (2018, April). Falling for fake news: investigating the consumption of news via social media. In *Proceedings of the 2018 CHI Conference on Human Factors in Computing Systems* (paper 376). New York, NY: Association for Computing Machinery.

Folk, H. (2017). "Cult crimes" and fake news: Eye-gouging in Shanxi. *The Journal of CESNUR, 1*(2), 96–109.

Goel, R., & Yadav, K. (2020). Poultry prices skid in India due to fake news circulation on coronavirus. https://osf.io/preprints/socarxiv/9gq6n/

Graham, D. (2019, June 7). Some real news about fake news. *Atlantic.* www.theatlantic.com/ideas/archive/2019/06/fake-news-republicans-democrats/591211/

Head, A., Wihbey, J., Metaxas, P., MacMillan, M., & Cohen, D. (2018). *How students engage with news: Five takeaways for educators, journalists, and librarians.* Chicago, IL: Association of College and Research Libraries.

Hirdman, A. (2019). Digital sociality, groups and the emotional imprint of algorithmic patterns. In U. Carlsson (Ed.), *Understanding media and information literacy (MIL) in the digital age: A question of democracy* (pp. 99–102). Gothenburg, Sweden: University of Gothenburg.

Hurley, M., & Smith, K. (2019). The Aviv report. In K. Smith & M. Hurley (Eds.), *I solemnly swear: Conmen, dea, and media and Pan Am 103* (pp. 116–132). Bloomington, IN: iUniverse.

Hutt, D. (2017, May 9). Fake news, real danger in Southeast Asia. *Asia Times*, 9.

Imhoff, R., & Lamberty, P. (2020). A bioweapon or a hoax? The link between distinct conspiracy beliefs about the Coronavirus disease (COVID-19) outbreak and pandemic behavior. https://doi.org/10.31234/osf.io/ye3ma

Ioannidis, J. P. (2020). Coronavirus disease 2019: The harms of exaggerated information and non-evidence-based measures. *European Journal of Clinical Investigation, 50*(4), e13222.

Ireton, C., & Posetti, J. (2018). *Journalism, "fake news" & disinformation.* Paris: UNESCO.

Jang, S. M., Geng, T., Li, J. Y. Q., Xia, R., Huang, C. T., Kim, H., & Tang, J. (2018). A computational approach for examining the roots and spreading patterns of fake news: Evolution tree analysis. *Computers in Human Behavior, 84*, 103–113.

Jang, S. M., & Kim, J. K. (2018). Third person effects of fake news: Fake news regulation and media literacy interventions. *Computers in Human Behavior, 80*, 295–302.

Kahneman, D. (2011). *Thinking, fast and slow.* New York, NY: Macmillan.

Kaufman, S. (2019, February 14). Liberals and conservatives are both susceptible to fake news, but for different reasons. *Scientific American.* https://blogs.scientificamerican.com/beautiful-minds/liberals-and-conservatives-are-both-susceptible-to-fake-news-but-for-different-reasons/

Kirtley, J. (2018). Getting to the truth: Fake news, libel laws, and "Enemies of the American people." *Human Rights, 43*(4), 6–9.

Kovach, B., & Rosenstiel, T. (2010). *Blur: How to know what's true in the age of information overload.* New York, NY: Bloomsbury.

Kriel, C. (2017). Fake news, fake wars, fake worlds. *Defence Strategic Communications, 3*(3), 171–190.

Kucharski, A. (2016). Post-truth: Study epidemiology of fake news. *Nature, 540*(7634), 525.

Lazer, D. M., Baum, M. A., Benkler, Y., Berinsky, A. J., Greenhill, K. M., Menczer, F., … & Schudson, M. (2018). The science of fake news. *Science, 359*(6380), 1094–1096.

Martens, B., Aguiar, L., Gómez, E., & Mueller-Langer, F. (2018). *The digital transformation of news media and the rise of disinformation and fake news.* Seville, Spain: Joint Research Centre.

McGrew, S., Ortega, T., Breakstone, J., & Wineburg, S. (2017). The challenge that's bigger than fake news: Civic reasoning in a social media environment. *American Educator, 41*(3), 4–9.

Mejova, Y., & Kalimeri, K. (2020). Advertisers jump on coronavirus bandwagon: Politics, news, and business. *arXiv* preprint arXiv:2003.00923.

Mellema, V. (2014, March 5). Do men use Facebook differently than women? *Social Media Today.* www.socialmediatoday.com/content/do-men-use-facebook-differently-women

Menczer, F. (2016, November 28). Fake online news spreads through social echo chambers. *The Conversation.* www.scientificamerican.com/article/fake-online-news-spreads-through-social-echo-chambers/

Meyer, R. (2018, March 8). The grim conclusions of the largest-ever study of fake news. *Atlantic.* www.theatlantic.com/technology/archive/2018/03/largest-study-ever-fake-news-mit-twitter/555104/

Mitchell, A., Gottferied, J., Barthel, M., & Sumida, N. (2018). *Distinguishing between factual and opinion statements in the news.* Washington, DC: Pew Research Center.

Mitchell, A., Gottfried, J., Stocking, G., Walker, M., & Fedeli, S. (2019). *Many Americans say made-up news is a critical problem that needs to be fixed.* Washington, DC: Pew Research Center.

Mukerjee, M. (2017, July 14). How fake news goes viral—here's the math. *Scientific American.* www.scientificamerican.com/article/how-fake-news-goes-viral-mdash-heres-the-math/Langer2/publication/325184841_The_Digital_Transformation_of_News_Media_and_the_Rise_of_Disinformation_and_Fake_News/links/5bfe74f0a6fdcc1b8d48700e/The-Digital-Transformation-of-News-Media-and-the-Rise-of-Disinformation-and-Fake-News.pdf

Nee, R. (2019). Youthquakes in a post-truth era: Exploring social media news use and information verification actions among global teens and young adults. *Journalism & Mass Communication Educator, 74*(2), 171–184.

Nelson, M. (2013). The hidden persuaders: Then and now. *Journal of Advertising, 37*(1), 113–126.

Newman, N., Fletcher, R., Kalogeropoulos, A., Levy, D., & Nielsen, R. K. (2017). *Reuters Institute digital news report 2017.* Oxford, UK: Reuters Institute.

Nielsen, R. K., Fletcher, R., Newman, N., Brennen, J. S., & Howard, P. N. (2020, April). Navigating the "infodemic": How people in six countries access and rate news and information about coronavirus. *British Time.* www.politico.eu/wp-content/uploads/2020/04/Navigating-the-Coronavirus-infodemic.pdf

O'Connor, C., & Weatherall, J. (2019). Why we trust lies. *Scientific American, 321*(3), 54–61.

Ohlsson, J., Lindell, J., & Arkhede, S. (2017). A matter of cultural distinction: News consumption in the online media landscape. *European Journal of Communication, 32*(2), 116–130.

Packard, V. (1957). *The hidden persuaders.* New York, NY: Longmans, Green & Co.

Pariser, E. (2011). *The filter bubble: What the Internet is hiding from you*. New York, NY: Penguin.

Pennycook, G., & Rand, D. G. (2019). Lazy, not biased: Susceptibility to partisan fake news is better explained by lack of reasoning than by motivated reasoning. *Cognition, 188*, 39–50.

Pestalardo, M. (2006). *War on the media: The news framing of the Iraqi War in the United States, Europe, and Latin America*. Master's thesis. East Tennessee State University.

Peters, A., Tartari, E., Lotfinejad, N., Parneix, P., & Pittet, D. (2018). Fighting the good fight: The fallout of fake news in infection prevention and why context matters. *Journal of Hospital Infection, 100*(4), 365–370.

Posetti, J., & Matthews, A. (2018). *A short guide to the history of "fake news" and disinformation*. Washington, DC: International Center for Journalists.

Pulido, C. M., Villarejo-Carballido, B., Redondo-Sama, G., & Gómez, A. (2020). COVID-19 infodemic: More retweets for science-based information on coronavirus than for false information. *International Sociology*. 0268580920914755.

Rainie, H., Anderson, J., & Albright, J. (2017). *The future of free speech, trolls, anonymity and fake news online*. Washington, DC: Pew Research Center.

Reilly, I. (2018). F for Fake: Propaganda! Hoaxing! Hacking! Partisanship! and Activism! in the fake news ecology. *The Journal of American Culture, 41*(2), 139–152.

Schramm, W. (1948). *Mass communication*. Urbana, IL: University of Illinois Press.

Schulman, R., & Siman-Tov, D. (2020). *From biological weapons to miracle drugs: Fake news about the coronavirus pandemic*. Pretoria, South Africa: Institute for Security Studies.

Scott-Railton, J., Marquis-Boire, M., Guarnieri, C., & Marschalek, M. (2015). *Packrat: Seven years of a South American threat actor*. Toronto, Ottawa: University of Toronto.

Shane, S. (2017, January 18). From headline to photograph, a fake news masterpiece. *The New York Times*. https://nyti.ms/2jyOcpR

Shao, C., Ciampaglia, G. L., Varol, O., Flammini, A., & Menczer, F. (2017, July 24). The spread of fake news by social bots. *arXiv* preprint arXiv:1707.07592, 96–104.

Silverman, C., Lytvynenko, J., & Kung, W. (2020, January 6). Disinformation for hire: How a new breed of PR firms is selling lies online. *BuzzFeed News*. www.buzzfeednews.com/article/craigsilverman/disinformation-for-hire-black-pr-firms

Spinney, L. (2017). How Facebook, fake news and friends are warping your memory. *Nature News, 543*(7644), 168.

Spohr, D. (2017). Fake news and ideological polarization: Filter bubbles and selective exposure on social media. *Business Information Review, 34*(3), 150–160.

Tandoc Jr., E. C., Ling, R., Westlund, O., Duffy, A., Goh, D., & Zheng Wei, L. (2018). Audiences' acts of authentication in the age of fake news: A conceptual framework. *New Media & Society, 20*(8), 2745–2763.

Tenenboim, O., & Cohen, A. (2015). What prompts users to click and comment: A longitudinal study of online news. *Journalism, 16*(2), 198–217.

Toggle, C. A. (1998). The bias toward finding bias in television news. *Communication Reports, 11*(1), 65–72.

Uberti, D. (2016, December 15). The real history of fake news. *Columbia Journalism Review*. www.cjr.org/special_report/fake_news_history.php

Van Dijk, T. A. (2006). Discourse and manipulation. *Discourse & Society, 17*(3), 359–383.

Vosoughi, S., Roy, D., & Aral, S. (2018). The spread of true and false news online. *Science, 359*(6380), 1146–1151.

Wasserman, H. (2017). Fake news from Africa: Panics, politics and paradigms. *Journalism, 18*, 1–14.

Yagoda, B. (2018, September). Your lying mind: The cognitive biases tricking your brain. *Atlantic, 322*(2), 72–80.

Yee, A. (2017). Post-truth politics & fake news in Asia. *Global Asia, 12*(2), 66–71.

Zhao, Z., Zhao, J., Sano, Y., Levy, O., Takayasu, H., Takayasu, M., … & Havlin, S. (2018). Fake news propagate differently from real news even at early stages of spreading. *arXiv* preprint arXiv:1803.03443.

3

THE DISCERNMENT CONTEXT

Some fake news is easy to spot, such as "Alien babys take over the wurld," but much fake news has become highly sophisticated in terms of believable content and professional look. Because fake news has the potential to influence daily life and major decisions, both end users and disseminators need to accurately identify fake news – and distinguish it from real news (Pearson, 2017).

Indeed, thinking that real news is fake can be as damaging as believing fake news because it still impacts people's attitudes and actions. Not believing in a real earthquake warning, for instance, can be life threatening. Some of the fallouts of the proliferation of fake news include cynicism, general distrust, and social withdrawal as people avoid news, both fake and real. Instead, those people limit their access to information, including different points of view, and thus may make uninformed decisions.

Fake news will endure, just as rumors and gossip have been part of human existence throughout history. As such, relying on media outlets and government entities to stop fake news is not realistic. Even if those groups *could* stop fake news, they are liable to make a mistake themselves occasionally and misinterpret a news item, censoring a potentially important piece of information (Andorfer, 2017; Jang & Kim, 2018). Even algorithms are limited because they are created by humans. No one has complete knowledge, so giving up the right to access and ascertain the validity of information is a dangerous decision for any person to make.

In the final analysis, everyone needs to learn how to discern fake news and real news.

Reviewing what is news

In order to evaluate the quality of news, one needs to understand what qualifies as news. As a reminder, news reports timely natural and human-made events that interest and impact the public. News usually piques people's interest if it is novel or surprising, features prominent people or events, or incites controversy. The news reporter – the journalist – also has a unique responsibility: to be fair and complete, to be independent from the news source so as not to be unduly influenced, and to apply judgment to information. In order to accomplish this task, the journalist needs to observe carefully and thoroughly, research the background and context of the news, employ and attribute credible primary and secondary sources, and organize the information in a thoughtful, incisive way to bring value to the news (Detrani, 2011).

Kovach and Rosenstiel (2010) listed the elements of an ideal news story: besides the story itself, they stated that every news event could include headlines, photographs, graphic or background information, a sidebar or analysis piece, and a sound bite. Kovach and Rosenstiel also asserted that websites can include several additional elements: interactive graphics and timelines, photo gallery, videos, interview transcripts, author biographies, means for crowdsourcing and sharing information, FAQs, and hyperlinks to associated terms, facts, sources and people.

Heuristics

It is impossible for anyone to read every bit of news thoroughly, even if limited to just the news that captures one's eye, not every news story that is broadcast 24/7. However, several heuristics, or aids or tips, can help uncover fake news. While many of these aids can apply to any source of information, the consumer can focus on the news elements when judging the information.

To help people remember those tips, heuristics sometimes use mnemonics or other memory aids. For instance, this simple "Look 4 ways" guide (Farmer, 2018) can be remembered kinesthetically, even by youngsters:

- Look through: read – or at least skim – the entire news story for its content, writing quality, appearance, consistency. The action is pointing fingers up and down.
- Look up: trace back to the source of the story and its image. The action is pointing fingers up.
- Look across: read other versions of the same news from other sources. The action is pointing fingers across and together.
- Look in: be mindful of your own biases and emotions, such as your immediate emotional reactions to the news, to determine if they affect judgment. The action is pointing fingers to yourself.

This heuristic provides a framework to examine other heuristics that can help uncover fake news.

Several heuristics have been developed, particularly by librarians, to evaluate websites. As mentioned before, the Internet facilitated an open universe of information. Up to that point, most information organizations, such as libraries, located and selected information sources that were reputable and relevant to their communities; they managed a "closed universe" of information. Since organizations could not control the entirety of information available on the Internet, they needed to help their communities learn how to evaluate information resources for themselves. The resultant techniques and the criteria generally work well when assessing a news story. A good collection of applicable heuristics targeted to K-12 education is maintained by school librarian Kathy Schrock: www.schrockguide.net/critical-evaluation.html

Probably the most popular heuristic in the United States is the CRAAP test, created by an academic librarian: currency, relevance, authority, accuracy and purpose (Blakeslee, 2004). In 2017 the International Federation of Library Associations and Institutions created an infographic that illustrates key criteria for evaluating news (www.ifla.org/publications/node/11174):

- Consider the source: to understand the source's mission and purpose.
- Read beyond the headlines: to understand the whole story.
- Check the authors: to see if they are real and credible.
- Assess supporting sources: to ensure they support claims.
- Check the publication date: to see if the news is relevant and current.
- Ask if it is a joke: is it satire or a parody?
- Review your own biases: to see if they affect your own judgment.
- Ask experts: to get confirmation from independent people with knowledge.

Beyond a cursory examination using these criteria, news consumers can drill down into the content detail. What is the tone of the communication: more factual or more emotional, more professional or more folksy, in-depth or shallow? What sources are cited? Few news stories provide a bibliography, but they should be able to state expert sources or factual events. It should be noted that even first-hand witnesses have a bias and a limited view, so multiple sources are needed to show a pattern of reliability. Even opinion should be backed up with credible evidence. Are arguments logical and credible? Are generalizations based on a large enough number of cases with well-controlled variables, or are they based on a few anecdotes? Is there an alternate explanation for a phenomenon than the one expressed? Is more than one point of view or perspective presented? And, finally, what information is missing that should be presented (Kovach & Rosenstiel, 2010)? In the process of evaluating news, consumers need to be reminded to distinguish between bad (poor-quality) news and fake news. The former usually does not try to mislead people; it just does a poor job of stating the facts and building a valid case.

Media literacy also provides a useful basis for discerning fake news as much news is channeled through mass media outlets. The Center for Media Literacy (2019) identified five research-based criteria for judging media messages:

- Authorship: who creates the message.
- Purpose: why is the message sent (e.g., to gain profit or power).

- Content: what ideas, viewpoints, lifestyles and values are included and omitted.
- Format: what format-specific techniques gain attention.
- Audience: how might different audiences understand the message.

Another aspect of news is its visual elements, which need to be evaluated from several dimensions (Carlson, 2009). First, artistic principles should be considered: balance, movement, rhythm, pattern and emphasis. Next, technical aspects should be examined: the quality and resolution of the image, and how the image has been manipulated: cropped, distorted and altered. For instance, if the DPI (dots per inch) varies within an image, it could well signal manipulation in that altered area. Then the image's content can be examined, both in itself and as it complements the text. A solid science background can also help identify illogical images such as sharks in swimming pools, a person standing straight upright while holding a hundred-pound animal, and exact replicas of natural objects such as wind tunnels. The same questions asked in terms of media fit here: intent, ideas and viewpoint. It is also important to determine the source of the image since news creators often draw upon other sources to provide the image and repurpose it, sometimes without crediting the source. Fortunately, now it is easier to trace an image's provenance by using image-tracking such as TinEye, Fotoforensics, Yandex (a Russian search engine) and Google Reverse Image Search. Additionally, analysis should determine how the images reinforce, extend, enrich, complement or even contradict the text. This interplay between text and image is called dual-modal discourse or dual-coding in that the semantic relationship builds meaning, and helps to comprehend and contextualize the news (Messaris & Abraham, 2001).

Sounds can be easily modified through audio-editing software that can edit words and modify pitch and pacing, along with changing the context of the audio source. Audio also comprises one of several "channels" in video-editing programs, so sounds can be edited separately or linked with the video channels. In either case, consumers can input an existing audio file into such editing software (e.g., Audacity, Acoustica, Studio, Audition), and see the spectrogram's graphic distortions. Even without editing expertise or access, consumers can trace a digital audio file by looking at the website's source code.

Moving images such as videos follow the same pattern as images and text, realizing that sound and movement add to the variables that need to be examined. Fake videos can be generated by combining and editing existing video to give a different "spin" or misleading message. Video manipulation has become more sophisticated and extensive; deepfakes, for instance, result from encoding and synthesizing existing and source media with apps that employ machine learning techniques. Particularly in politics, such deepfakes can misrepresent public figures in very convincing footage. As with audio files, viewers can examine video files on video-editing software such as Premiere, Camtasia, Studio 16 and Filmora. Likewise, they can look at a website's source code if the video is embedded in it. Algorithms are also being developed to identify fake videos by detecting anomalies such as irregular patterns of lighting or color. Dartmouth College computer scientist Hany

Farid, who specializes in detecting manipulated images, including video, provides this detection service to educational and media organizations (Gibney, 2017). Africa Check used crowdsourcing on Twitter to verify that a video was fake because the airplane being cited never reached an altitude high enough to deploy the oxygen masks shown in the video (Funke, 2019).

Manual fact-checkers

With practice – and increasing life experience and growing knowledge base – people can improve their fact-checking skills: that is, verifying the authenticity and accuracy of news. However, with the proliferation of news encountered every day, people can feel daunted by the idea of checking every bit of possible fake news. Indeed, fact-checking is a time-consuming and intellectually challenging effort, not for the faint-hearted. To uncover possible fake news, people increasingly depend on fact-checking tools and fact-checkers.

The need for checking the veracity of information is not new. Professional journalism fact-checkers have existed for a century, originally checking facts and figures before publication and then extending those skills to fact-check ex-post political media (Mantzarlis, 2018). What distinguishes professional fact-checkers from amateurs? For one thing, professional fact-checkers have deep content knowledge; in that respect, many fact-checkers are subject area specialists, which works well for large enterprises that provide fact-checking services. As such, they research the background and context of the news. They also compare other treatments of the same news event. As skillful communicators, professional fact-checkers also carefully analyze the quality and tone of the news for professional practice (Uscinski & Butler, 2013).

Even with their expertise, professional fact-checkers do not always agree in their assessment of the veracity of news. Obvious truths, blatant lies and straight facts are relatively easy to discern. However, when the language is ambiguous or subtly builds on true statements, or when the supporting evidence itself is very controversial such as charter schools, fact-checkers sometimes disagree on the news' quality or how to interpret the information (Lim, 2018). Additionally, media outlets try to balance accuracy with openness and pluralism; for example, different political parties might have different perspectives on how to govern, but they each may have valid points, which should be reported (Graves & Cherubini, 2016).

Nevertheless, fact-checking is an important responsibility, and fact-checking enterprises have offered useful services for years. As early as 1994, Snopes.com pointed out urban legends and other incredible stories. Focusing on serious political issues, FactCheck.org began in 2003, followed by PolitiFact in 2007. With the proliferation of fake news, fact-checking has become a viable industry in itself, increasing from 44 organizations in 2014 to 195 in 2019. At the same time, these organizations are tending to separate themselves from traditional journalism outlets. Furthermore, fact-checking organizations may have different intents and perspectives, so even they need to be evaluated for their credibility (Bell, 2019). The International Fact-Checking Network (2020) at Poynter developed a code of principles to promote excellent fact-checking. These principles include a commitment to:

- Nonpartisanship and fairness.
- Transparency of sources.
- Transparency of funding and organization.
- Transparency of methodology.
- Open and honest corrections policy.

Fact-checking organizations can apply to be a signatory to this code, and the network reviews that organization's news practices. As of 2020, 71 such organizations around the world have been approved as signatories, and are listed at https://ifcncodeofprinciples.poynter.org/signatories.

One variation of human fact-checking is leveraging collective intelligence through crowdsourced methods to detect fake news. The idea behind crowdsourcing is the belief that a heterogenous group of experts can arrive at a consensus about the validity of news. Kim et al. (2018) described a representative model process. In a social network site, a user flags a story as misinformation; if enough people flag the same story, a trusted third party fact-checks it, and marks it as disputed. Fiskkit employs another crowdsourcing model; it allows users to discuss and annotate the accuracy of news article sections (Shu et al., 2017). According to Funke (2019), keys to crowdsourcing success include initial independent judgment, subject expert justification of a stance, tech platform partnership, and mutual trust.

Automated fact-checking

While manual fact-checking continues to be used, the volume of news almost requires that some kind of automated processes be used to handle the flood. The concept is that computational methods can decrease the time between a false claim is published and a correction is made. Furthermore, automated processes can cut down on labor expense. Several organizations have designed algorithmic fact-checking tools (Hassan et al., 2017). Indeed, Google has given grants to support artificial intelligence (AI) efforts to automate fact-checking. However, few tools have reached the marketable stage. Understanding how automated fact-checking tools work helps people realize the complexity of identifying fake news accurately as well as consume news more knowledgably.

One technology-based way to detect fake news is through data mining, which can reveal patterns that distinguish between reliable news and disinformation. Those patterns can then be used to create a predictive model that can be translated into an algorithm for automated detection of fake news. Shu et al. (2017) mined several fake news detection data sets (BuzzFeedNews, PolitiFact, GossipCop, BS

Detector and CREDBANK) to extract features that could distinguish between real and fake news. In examining the content, the researchers used a knowledge-based approach by comparing the news with other external sources, and then utilized a style-based approach by identifying deceptive phrases and hyperpartisan style. The researchers also employed social context models that were stance-based (e.g., "likes"), propagation-based (e.g., the degree that social media networks are homogeneous).

In another study, by Gupta et al. in 2013, tweeted photos of Hurricane Sandy and its impact were analyzed to ascertain traits of faked images. The researchers used characterization analysis to identify time-based, social reputation and influence patterns. About 86 percent of the faked images were retweets rather than original tweets, and 30 users out of the more than 10,000 users comprised 90 percent of the fake image tweets. Next a decision tree classifier predicted the false images 97 percent of the time, based on tweet features: number of works, punctuation marks, use of capitals, pronoun use, positive and negative words.

A study conducted by Pérez-Rosas et al. (2018) helps to understand how an automated system might compare with a human fact-checking effort. To build an accurate fake news detector, the researchers created two data sets of false news, one collected via crowdsourcing for six news domains and the other collected directly from the websites that covered fake news about celebrities. The data sets included text-only news that could be true or false but having some ground truth, published within a pre-set timeframe for the same general purpose, with similar writing styles and article length. Each story was manually checked and categorized as either true or false. Then the researchers extracted several linguistic features: punctuation, readability, syntax, grammar, number of words per sentence, and emotional terms to use as the distinguishing variables. These variables were then classified through machine learning. Key variables that identified fake news included more social and positive words, more verbs and adverbs, more punctuation marks, a greater sense of certainty, and a focus on present and future action. In politics, education and technology domains, the researchers' best performing algorithmic model identified fake news as well as humans, but humans outperformed the model for celebrity and entertainment news.

Compared with human fact-checking, automated algorithms are more limited because they lack contextual knowledge to determine meaning. In that respect, the tool UnbiasedCrowd serves as an interesting model that leverages automated results to help human fact-checkers (Narwal et al., 2017). This Twitter tool uses Google's image search algorithm to collect images of a news story, and then the researchers use standard computer vision techniques to cluster similar images. The resultant image clusters help the viewer to more easily detect visual faked or biased images. Nevertheless, algorithms used to discern fake news are influenced by human biases as content and its use is self-selected in light of biases, and that can seed the data sets that are the basis for algorithms. To counteract such algorithm biases, developers have to recognize biases and readjust those algorithms accordingly (Baeza-Yates, 2018).

Comparing news sources

Checking the validity of each individual news article is labor-intensive; being able to depend on a news outlet in general saves much time and stress. Indeed, one of the advantages of a news outlet such as a newspaper, magazine or television news show is that the staff gathers, evaluates, selects and organizes a set of news stories that they think are newsworthy and interesting to their audience. Furthermore, many news outlets have a particular perspective or bent, which informs the reader.

In addition, the journalism organization NewsGuard (www.newsguardtech.com) uses nine journalistic criteria to assess news outlets' credibility and transparency:

- Does not publish false content repeatedly.
- Gathers and presents information responsibly using multiple sources, preferably with first-hand knowledge.
- Regularly corrects or clarifies errors.
- Handles the difference between news and opinion responsibly.
- Avoids deception, such as distorted headlines.
- Discloses organization's ownership and financing.
- Discloses who is in charge, and possible conflicts of interest.
- Names content creators, and provides contact of biographical information.
- Clearly labels advertising.

These journalistic criteria can help consumers determine the validity and reliability of a news outlet. To get a holistic view of the news being broadcast by any one outlet, uncovering patterns in the content and approach, here are some guiding steps:

1. Read the mission of the news outlet. News organizations typically have a mission statement or "about" page. Does the mission align with journalistic principles?
2. Uncover the sponsor of the news publication or broadcast. What people own the outlet? Who provides the financial backing? How dependent are they on advertisers? The publication's masthead or "about" page usually provides this information. This information can reveal the outlet's influencers and possible agenda.
3. Get an overview of a couple of issues or episodes of the news publication or broadcast. Flip through the issue, read the table of contents, watch the show trailer. What news gets priority, which is usually the lead story? What is the average length of a news story, and to what degree does the length vary between stories or sections of the broadcast or publication? What percentage of news stories are original versus stories that come from outside news services such as Reuters or AP; are those services noted? To what degree are news stories signed and their sources attributed? What topics are covered the most and least; what is omitted? What is the balance between straight reporting

(strictly informational) and opinion pieces (analysis and interpretation)? What is the balance between images and text? What is the balance between news and advertisements? Are the issues or episodes consistent in coverage and treatment?

4. Analyze an issue or episode in depth. What is the writing style and tone? What is the perspective; what political, ideological or cultural worldview is presented? Whose "voices" are communicated, and whose voices are left out? To what degree does the news story include background information; what sources are cited? To what degree does an opinion piece include evidence for its stance, and what is the quality of that evidence?

5. Analyze the images. What information do the images provide? What reaction do the images evoke? Do they reinforce or complement the text; do they contradict the text? What is the visual quality of the images? Is the source of each of the images attributed? What is the balance between original images and those that come from an outside news service?

6. Examine the advertisements. What is being sold? Who is the intended audience? How do the advertisements align with the news stories and their perspective? What political ads, if any, are shown, and what stances do they take? What social issues, if any, are represented in advertisements, and what stances do they take? Some news publications or broadcasts omit advertisements altogether as a symbol of independent reporting.

As noted previously, most news organizations or publications have a fairly consistent stance or perspective. Nevertheless, strong newspaper and news magazine brands attract broad audiences across the spectrum. For example, the BBC, the *New York Times*, the Associated Press, NPR, *Le Monde,* the *Australian*, AllAfrica. com, NDTV (Indian) are all highly reputable news sources worldwide. Professor Maxwell Stearns produced a multiple-analyst-generated media bias chart of major news outlets in the United States, which assesses media reliability and media bias: www.adfontesmedia.com/the-multiple-analyst-generated-media-bias-chart-by-professor-maxwell-stearns/. Similar charts could be produced for other countries and languages, as well as for specific subject areas such as science or religious news outlets. This kind of comparative chart provides a starting point for comparing news outlets in general, and for selecting a good balance of reputable sources for a daily diet of news.

Another good practice is to compare the same news story from differing perspectives or contexts. To that end, a couple of websites present multiple sources side by side in order to provide the full scope of news reporting:

- AllSides (United States): www.allsides.com/unbiased-balanced-news
- NewsCompare (United States): https://newscompare.com/
- Blue Feed, Red Feed (Facebook posts that are now archived): https://graphics. wsj.com/blue-feed-red-feed/

A similar website, Echo Chamber/Ekokammaren (https://ekokammaren.se/), from Sweden provides similar comparisons, following the Blue Feed, Red Feed model. That service was in abeyance for a while because Facebook has made it considerably hard to access data and develop tools such as Ekokammaren, partly due to the Cambridge Analytica leak. In discussing Ekokammaren, creator Martin Törnros noted the "two sides of the coins when it comes to public social media data access: integrity versus civic technology restrictions."

Just as an individual news story can be analyzed, so too can the criteria be employed to reveal differences in news coverage and accuracy: thoroughness of the content and context, sources of information, writing style and tone, degree of analysis and interpretation, and point of view. In addition, learning how different cultures and governments view a news story, or how information is falsified, can help people better understand how misunderstandings can arise – and, hopefully, how to bridge differences.

A note about culture

Culture poses an additional factor in discerning fake news. At the least, when audiences encounter news from a different culture – be it social, political or ideological – they may misinterpret the news because they do not understand the assumptions or communication styles of people unlike themselves. Terms, especially idioms, may have different connotations, some of them serious in implications in different cultures. Seemingly objective words such as "swipe," "snatch," and "dog" have totally different meanings in different contexts. Each culture has unique speech patterns and tones that might be aggressive, jarring or be misinterpreted by a different culture. Sensitive and taboo subjects are socially defined, and fake news can leverage such controversies to insight anger or polarization between cultures. Even some images might be considered insensitive or inappropriate in some cultures, which may evoke negative feelings impacting the viewer's attitude and action. Especially when fake news is disseminated without context or human interaction, fewer cues are provided to clarify sometimes very ambiguous meaning (Holtbrügge et al., 2011).

The above aspects of culture assume at least a modicum of openness or neutral ignorance. If the news is created or broadcast from an opposing culture (or framed as if coming from the oppositional group), there may be an automatic disapproving or skeptical reaction. Audiences need to assess their own cultural biases to determine if the news triggers possible negative emotions that are not fact based. In general, fake news comes from a locus of power where it is thought that the real news might threaten existing power structures; their fake news provides a counter narrative that tries to squelch that uprising. Usually such actions assume that power is a win-lose sum game rather than an open-ended inclusion of different powers. This kind of mind shift can be difficult for some people to accept. On the other hand, when marginalized or oppressed groups think that they have no voice or "buy-in" into the existing social structure, they may feel that they have little to lose if they react more physically or violently to their present conditions. Therefore, giving them opportunities to voice counter narratives offers an escape valve and a way to engage in public discourse that can influence significant action (Kahne, Hodgin & Eidman-Aadahl, 2016). As a consumer, it is important to position one's own perspective, realizing possible biases that might distort news reception. Even if the news is uncomfortable, it might be more truthful than the fake news that confirms pre-existing prejudices (McGrew et al., 2017).

No easy answers exist in uncovering and accurately interpreting cultural connotations. However, consumers can be aware of the potential of misunderstanding news because of cultural differences. Identifying the source of the news is a good first step. Does that information truly originate from the source, or is another entity disguising itself as the altercating group? What is the agenda of that culture: to express its own stance, educate the audience, to persuade, to provoke, to mislead? In the final analysis, understanding more about other cultures, their communication styles and values, helps consumers maintain an open mind when trying to interpret the validity of news from other cultures.

In sum

In the final analysis, all of these strategies to discern fake news should be examined in light of one's own self-awareness, knowledge and context. What are one's own experiences, situations and biases that may trigger personal reactions to different news, including fake news? After all, the main basis for disinformation and fake news is humans. Cultural biases become shared personal beliefs, and cognitive biases rise from reactions to experiences. Both of these types of biases impact the creation, dissemination and discernment of fake news (Ciampaglia & Menczer, 2018). Fortunately, several heuristics and tools are available to help individuals address the objectivity and validity of news – and their reactions to news.

References

Andorfer, A. (2017). Spreading like wildfire: Solutions for abating the fake news problem on social media via technology controls and government regulation. *Hastings Law Journal*, *69*(5), 1409–1431.

Baeza-Yates, R. (2018). Bias on the Web. *Communications of the ACM*, *61*(6), 54–61.

Bell, E. (2019). The fact-check industry. *Columbia Journalism Review*, *58*(3), 48–52.

Blakeslee, S. (2004). The CRAAP test. *LOEX Quarterly*, *31*(3), 4.

Carlson, M. (2009). The reality of a fake image: News norms, photojournalistic craft, and Brian Walski's fabricated photograph. *Journalism Practice*, *3*(2), 125–139.

Center for Media Literacy. (2019). *MediaLit kit*. Santa Monica, CA: Center for Media Literacy.

Ciampaglia, G., & Menczer, F. (2018, June 21). Biases make people vulnerable to misinformation spread by social media. *Scientific American*. https://theconversation.com/misinformation-and-biases-infect-social-media-both-intentionally-and-accidentally-97148

Detrani, J. (2011). *Journalism: Theory and practice*. Boca Raton, FL: CRC Press.

Farmer, L. (2018). Fake news is now ubiquitous. *The Catholic Library World*, *89*(2), 96.

Funke, D. (2019, March 14). Is expert crowdsourcing the solution to health misinformation? *Poynter.* www.poynter.org/fact-checking/2019/is-expert- crowdsourcing-the-solution-to-health-misinformation/

Gibney, E. (2017, October 6). The scientist who spots fake videos. *Nature News.* https://doi.org/10.1038/nature.2017.22784

Graves, L., & Cherubini, F. (2016). *The rise of fact-checking sites in Europe.* Oxford, UK: Reuters Institute.

Gupta, A., Lamba, H., Kumaraguru, P., & Joshi, A. (2013, May). Faking Sandy: Characterizing and identifying fake images on Twitter during Hurricane Sandy. In *Proceedings of the 22nd International Conference on World Wide Web* (pp. 729–736). New York, NY: Association for Computing Machinery.

Hassan, N., Zhang, G., Arslan, F., Caraballo, J., Jimenez, D., Gawsane, S., … & Sable, V. (2017). Claimbuster: The first-ever end-to-end fact-checking system. *Proceedings of the VLDB Endowment, 10*(12), 1945–1948.

Holtbrügge, D., Schillo, K., Rogers, H., & Friedmann, C. (2011). Managing and training for virtual teams in India. *Team Performance Management, 17*(3), 206–223.

International Fact-Checking Network. (2018). *Code of principles.* St. Petersburg, FL: Poynter.

Jang, S. M., & Kim, J. K. (2018). Third person effects of fake news: Fake news regulation and media literacy interventions. *Computers in Human Behavior, 80,* 295–302.

Kahne, J., Hodgin, E., & Eidman-Aadahl, E. (2016). Redesigning civic education for the digital age: Participatory policies and the pursuit of democratic engagement. *Theory & Research in Social Education, 44*(1), 1–35.

Kim, J., Tabibian, B., Oh, A., Schölkopf, B., & Gomez-Rodriguez, M. (2018). Leveraging the crowd to detect and reduce the spread of fake news and misinformation. In *Proceedings of the Eleventh ACM International Conference on Web Search and Data Mining* (pp. 324–332). New York, NY: Association for Computing Machinery.

Kovach, B., & Rosenstiel, T. (2010). *Blur.* New York, NY: Bloomsburg.

Lim, C. (2018). Checking how fact-checkers check. *Research & Politics, 5*(3), 1–7.

Mantzarlis, A. (2018). Module 5: Fact-checking 101. In C. Ireton & J. Posetti (Eds.), *Journalism, fake news & disinformation* (pp. 81–95). Paris, France: UNESCO.

McGrew, S., Ortega, T., Breakstone, J., & Wineburg, S. (2017). The challenge that's bigger than fake news: Civic reasoning in a social media environment. *American Educator, 41*(3), 4–9.

Messaris, P., & Abraham, L. (2001). The role of images in framing news stories. In S. Reese, O. Gandy, Jr., & A. Grant (Eds.), *Framing public life* (pp. 231–242). New York, NY: Routledge.

Narwal, V., Salih, M. H., Lopez, J. A., Ortega, A., O'Donovan, J., Höllerer, T., & Savage, S. (2017). Automated assistants to identify and prompt action on visual news bias. In *Proceedings of the 2017 CHI Conference Extended Abstracts on Human Factors in Computing Systems* (pp. 2796–2801). New York, NY: Association of Computer Machinery.

NewsGuard. (2020). *Rating process and criteria.* New York, NY: NewsGuard.

Pearson, M. (2017, July 18). Teaching media law in a post-truth context: Strategies for enhancing learning about the legal risks of fake news and alternative facts. *Asia Pacific Media Educator, 27*(1), 17–26.

Pérez-Rosas, V., Kleinberg, B., Lefevre, A., & Mihalcea, R. (2018, August). Automatic detection of fake news. In *Proceedings of the 27th International Conference on Computational Linguistics* (pp. 3391–3401). Stroudsburg, PA: Association for Computational Linguistics.

Shu, K., Sliva, A., Wang, S., Tang, J., & Liu, H. (2017). Fake news detection on social media: A data mining perspective. *ACM SIGKDD Explorations Newsletter, 19*(1), 22–36.

Uscinski, J. E., & Butler, R. W. (2013). The epistemology of fact checking. *Critical Review, 25*(2), 162–180.

4

THE RESPONSIBILITY CONTEXT

Whose job is it to address fake news? The communications cycle model provides a framework to identify responsible parties and their social responsibilities: subject experts, news creators, disseminators, communications broadcasters, government agencies, consumers, educators and other information professionals.

Subject experts

Each field and industry sector have their experts. While some information is important only to internal personnel, other information is shared with the public in order to inform or influence them. For example, scientists want to warn the public about global warming, doctors want to explain about the importance of vaccinations, businesses want to give investment advice, architects want to give advice about earthquake preparedness, academicians want to share the latest theoretical research. As professionals, they are likely to have, and comply with, codes of ethics that guide their practice. Such ethics points out the importance of truthfulness in researching and communicating knowledge.

Communication issues impact fake news for subject experts. First, professionals tend to communicate with their peers rather than with the general public, the idea being that peers can advance the knowledge base more effectively than laymen. In that process, they tend to use professional lingo and do not have to explain domain-specific concepts. Even within that arena, professionals need to encourage open sources to speed up dissemination and peer review. Beyond that measure, subject experts have a responsibility to convey the impact of their research findings to non-experts. Communicating with the general public requires disseminating information through popular mainstream media outlets and social media. Secondly, as subject experts communicate with the general public, they need to provide clear and understandable explanations, use jargon-free and non-technical vocabulary, and simplify without over-generalizing. In that respect, visualizing data in infographics and creating videos can help comprehension; communication skills that some experts need to gain (Ngumbi, 2019).

In communicating research emerges the issue of directly confronting fake news. Even journalists with professional training and credentials can misinterpret research, which means that they should have subject experts review their stories to verify the interpretation. More generally, people will deny expert authority if those same experts baldly accuse the fake news believer of illogic or assert that the fake news really is fallacious. Especially if the fake news precedes the accurate news and the false information affirms the consumers' deeply held values, those consumers will hold on even more tightly to their false beliefs and attack or denigrate the expert (Berinsky, 2015). Instead, experts need to avoid challenging the fake news or the fake news believer, and instead pose a coherent and compelling counter narrative (Khaldarova & Pantti, 2016). For example, instead of stating that vaccinations should be required, doctors can share narratives about the ramifications of not vaccinating, such as children suffering from preventative illness. Nevertheless, since the first news is the one that tends to be more influential, subject experts should try to pub- licize accurate news quickly, before fake news is written. This pre-emptive strike against falsehoods acts as an effective preventative measure against false news (Ortiz, 2018). On the other hand, preliminary scientific information may be incomplete, as was the case for the COVID-19 pandemic, which led to false impressions that were hard to overcome.

Journalists

Journalism is sometimes called the fourth estate because of its role in democracy as an independent source of information for citizens and their government. The term "estate" separates it linguistically from the three branches of government (legis- lative, executive and judicial). Rusbridger (2018) asserted that "reporters are the bees of the world's information systems" (p. 378) as they spread news to pollinate society. Journalism is both more powerful and yet more precarious in the digital age. Journalists have more ways to access information, but have more competition from communication channels that do not use journalists. Journalists are held to high expectations at the same time that their news organizations have decreased the number of staff and resources as well as tightened deadlines to support those high expectations. Journalists are asked to be transparent, but then valuable sources are more reluctant to provide information. The stakes are higher than ever as poor- quality journalism allows fake news and other disinformation to be leaked or broad- cast; their reputations are on the line. At the same time, journalists are targets for complaints and harm (Ireton & Posetti, 2018). In Southeast Asia, for instance, some governments use Facebook as an instrument to intensify censorship of journalists and to harass mainstream media outlets (Hutt, 2017).

The state of journalism education is uneven at best, and tends to have a Western perspective, which undervalues approaches of non-Western societies. Nevertheless, journalists around the world agree that journalism should encompass accurate observation, selection of newsworthy stories, ethical processing and editing of those stories, and effective distribution of news (Goodman & Steyn, 2017). In any case, for journalists to report news effectively, they need to be information literate themselves. In an age of fake news, Bobkowski and Younger (2019) detailed the desired journalistic workflow relative to gathering information. Their premise was that information is only as credible as the journalist's sources. The two authors recommended several useful practices: search and re-search for information, use search operators effectively, evaluate information rigorously, search again later based on the initial cues and evidence already collected, manage the information gathered by keeping detailed research notes and their attributions. In terms of casting a wide net to gather information, the authors suggested leveraging the Freedom of Information Act to access open public records, accessing public records of companies, analyzing marketing research, connecting with trade associations and professional organizations, reading the scholarship research, digging into archives, checking out nonprint materials such as videos and podcasts, consulting the gray literature, interviewing experts, and tapping into credibility networks.

Similarly to writing journalists, photojournalists (for both still and moving pictures) should aim to convey an accurate and thorough account of the news they cover. Therefore, they too need to be information literate in terms of ensuring that their sources are reliable and valid. In addition, they need to be visually literate to ensure that the images tell a truthful story, not one that misleads or manipulates the viewer. For instance, a camera angle can connote the presence or lack of the filmed person's power. Lighting can evoke feelings of confidence or suspicion. Timing can catch a politician using a commanding or awkward gesture. Sometimes photographers aim more for esthetics or spectacle than for accurate conveying of the news; because images contribute to meaning, and provide context for interpretation, photojournalists need to take their professional responsibility seriously (Carlson, 2009; Messaris & Abraham, 2001).

Post-production can also distort the image's message, so photojournalists need to be technically literate at that stage as well as in the original shooting. Cropping an image can mislead the viewer; for instance, a thinly attended event can seem like a crowded one if an image is tightly cropped, and carefully cropped crowd scenes can show just happy faces – or disgruntled ones. Traditional development of film could impact the image quality and manipulate the image itself to a limited extent; today's digital cameras greatly expand the possibilities for image editing and manipulation. Nowadays, images from different sources can be combined and remixed, which is hard for the viewer to perceive (Gibney, 2017).

Even with the best sources, news depends on journalists' own experiences, attitudes and values (Toggle, 1998). Not only should news organizations report the news in an accurate and fair way; they should practice ethical behavior. Journalists have much potential power because they choose what news to convey and what to omit; they need to be mindful of their own biases so as to not convey those biases in their photographic efforts but rather aim to a diversity of viewpoints. Interestingly, the concept of journalistic objectivity is a relatively recent idea, yet is now the public's normal expectation (Haigh, Haigh & Kozak, 2018). To the credit of the journalism profession, it should be noted that most Americans do not blame journalists for the most part in creating fake news, but they put much of the responsibility for *fixing* fake news on journalists (Mitchell et al., 2019). In that respect, history does have an important lesson to tell. Yellow journalism, with its sensationalism and its own version of fake news, was in full swing in the late 19th century. Much of the public saw through the hype and mistrusted newspapers. A tension built up between public interest in good reporting and private profit. In the midst of this problem, the *New York Times* rose in reputation and profit because of its conservative, straight news. Additionally, in response to the unscrupulous newspaper practices, newspaper journalists developed a code of ethics (Samuel, 2016).

The current code of the Society of Professional Journalists (2014) guides journalism practice. Their society's four principles follow, focusing on indicators that impact on fake news.

- See truth and report it: be accountable and fair, which entails being honest and courageous in gathering, reporting and interpreting news.
- Minimize harm: respect all beings, balancing the public's need for information against potential discomfort or harm.
- Act independently: avoid conflicts of interest and other actions that may damage credibility.
- Be accountable and transparent: explain ethical processes to audiences, acknowledge and correct mistakes, and expose unethical journalistic behavior.

Among those indicators is an admonishment that speed and format do not excuse inaccuracy, and that journalists should support open and civil exchange of views, even those that seem repugnant.

Focusing on post-print open journalism, Rusbridger (2018) and colleagues suggested the following principles.

- Be open-minded about the Internet, and be part of it; link to other websites.
- Encourage participation and response.
- Avoid static news.
- Allow pre-production initiation and involvement by non-journalists.
- Form communities of interest.
- Try to promote shared values and reflect diversity.
- Aggregate and curate information from other published works.
- Realize that an existing published story may be the beginning of a journalistic process, not just the end point.
- Realize that journalists are not the only voices of authority or expertise.
- Practice transparency and be open to challenges.

A subset of journalists, photojournalists have their own code of ethics (National Press Photographers Association, 2019). While a number of their standards duplicate the generic journalists' standards, a few address visual messages explicitly.

- Develop a unique vision and presentation, and continue to develop professionally.
- Resist staged photo opportunity manipulation.
- Avoid stereotyping.
- Respect all subjects, and be particularly considerate of victims (e.g., record private grief only when there is a justifiable need for the public to see it). Try to be unobtrusive.
- Avoid in-camera or post-editing that alters or influences events.
- Do not sabotage or harass colleagues and other journalists; defend the right of access for all journalists.

Journalism codes of ethics constitute one aspect of maintaining a trusting relationship with news audiences, which helps deter skepticism about news in general, caused by the fact that social media enables almost anyone to publish news. To build trust, journalists do well to explain to their audience about their ethical standards and how they maintain them in their professional practice. As an example, the *New York Times* now includes a special section that fact-checks public statements and encourages readers to avoid taking information at face value blindly. API publishes a weekly e-newsletter, "Trust Tips," that highlights ethical practices and trust-building efforts. The staff of the website Trusting News (http://trustingnews.org) studies how people decide which news to trust in order to help journalists employ trust-building strategies (Keiser, 2019). The Global Editors Network developed a European media literacy toolkit for newsrooms (www.globaleditorsnetwork.org/programmes/the-media-literacy-toolkit/) to facilitate understanding between journalists and citizens.

Some schools partner with local news outlets to teach news and media literacy (Muratova & Grizzle, 2019). At this point, more than 50 countries have some type of "newspaper in education" program, which include student materials and professional development (Hobbs, 2016). As service learning has become more prevalent in schools, students are given more opportunities to shadow journalists out in the field, serving as junior reporters and collaborating in publishing student newspapers (Stakston, 2019). Youth particularly like interactivity that is the result of co-production, where they participate in producing and manipulating information, balanced with professional mentoring and monitoring. This kind of partnership can jumpstart citizen journalism. Citizen journalism may be defined as user-centered news production and participatory journalism, which is often associated with social media. In this environment, youth respond well when given responsibilities to serve their communities, which leads to more positive personal development (Bennett, 2008).

Even with these efforts, journalists face challenges that yellow journalists did not face over a century before: an expanded base of news creators, many more media formats and channels, greater and faster access to news, and much easier ways to share real and fake news. The problem has become much more complex, and more stakeholders need to play a role in addressing and stemming fake news.

Nevertheless, journalists have an inside track to report on fake news and ways to address it. As media and information literacy is a key way to discern fake news, UNESCO's guide on media and information literacy for journalists (Muratova & Grizzle, 2019) asserted that journalists should do the following practices:

- Investigate and report on the role of media and information literacy in education, government and society.
- Investigate and report on research about the impact of media and information literacy on citizens and societies.
- Report on media outlets' promotion of media and information literacy and its impact on the relationship between the media outlets and their audiences.
- Report on media and information literacy policies.

To that end, Keiser (2019) has documented several initiatives by journalists to address fake news. For instance, the American Press Institute's Accountability Journalism and Fact-Checking Project publishes a weekly update of groups combating misinformation. The project also maintains a free fact-checking resource page, Better News, which explains fact-checking and its tactics; among its resources is a free online course (www.poynter.org/shop/fact-checking/handson-factchecking/). These approaches reflect a sense of civic journalism, with an obligation to the public beyond just reporting, but rather fostering public discourse to validate community members and their contributions to the world of news (Frechette, 2016).

Media outlets

Media outlets – be they newspaper publishers, television stations or blogs – select, curate and disseminate news. The outlet's own staff might do the reporting or production, use news agencies such as Reuters or Associated Press, outsource the news source, or just draw from other communications channels such as social media. Their power lies in choosing which news to cover and how to treat that news. That treatment can vary along several dimensions: length of the story, type of story (e.g., informational, analytical, opinion piece), contextual or affiliated aspects (e.g., images, side bars, graphs, back stories, interviews, hyperlinks), placement (e.g., priority feature, sequence order, layout location). In short, media outlets shape information, resulting in infrastructural meaning-making that can then influence how their audiences view the world (Haider & Sundin, 2019).

As noted above, reporters have the responsibility for gathering the news, researching the news' context, checking their sources, and writing it up as "copy."

They may also analyze and interpret the news. Photo or video journalists may accompany the reporters. Editors edit the copy, and decide which news (and which formats) to include in their issue and where to place the items. Television and radio news organizations typically use anchors or hosts to deliver the news.

At each step in mainstream media outlets, decisions are usually made collectively, with several checks and balances. Such collective oversight helps to counter extremism and fake news as each stakeholder justifies his or her stance, based on verified evidence. The major challenge to such practice is time, when facts are not checked and supervisors assume their employees will always act prudently, a situation that is exacerbated with staff cutbacks. Especially if the fake news is approved at the first step, it is likely to slip through the monitoring process the rest of the way. Due diligence is always required, even in the face of possibly delaying or missing a deadline. Increasingly, automated fact-checking tools may be used as a first line of defense to speed up the workflow, especially as fake news seems to travel faster than real news, but media outlets always need to be mindful of the limitations of algorithms.

Such shortcut practices are acerbated as media outlets, especially traditionally print newspapers, move into the online environment. Opinion pieces can transform into blogs, page views from database versions of news articles can be replaced by cost per click, directory and database indexing of newspapers can be tagged instead, and publishing can become more participatory – and perhaps less trustworthy (Rusbridger, 2018).

These efforts are especially important these days as unethical entities create faux local news websites. Knowing that people tend to trust local media outlets more than national or even regional outlets, biased groups sprinkle fake news in the midst of local school and sports coverage. Political figures have even been known to pay these ersatz local news sites to feature damaging fake news about their opponents. The target local readers tend to generalize the trustworthiness of the news and spread the false news among their neighbors. Such readers can "suss" out the faux news source by examining professional news practices such as mastheads and signed articles; fake news websites tend to omit such transparent features (Coppins, 2020).

The entire news organization sector needs to work transparently and ethically to gain and maintain public trust. Such professionalism is also good for business as increased trust increases readership and loyalty. In the Reuters Institute 2017 digital news report, the researchers (Newman et al., 2017) discovered that trust in news organizations varies by country. The highest trust level was found to exist in Finland, and the lowest level of trust was evidenced in Greece and South Korea. The highest perceived media bias was noted in the United States, Italy and Hungary.

Other efforts used to build trust include revealing their ownership or financial source, giving their audiences a voice in editorial or business decisions, and going out into the community to train them about journalism practices (Schiffrin, Santa-Wood & De Martino, 2019). In the same vein, France Television presents and explains different aspects of journalism, including the pace of production, which has improved the public's expectations (Muratova & Grizzle, 2019). As a further example, Angelina Jolie, Microsoft Education and BBC co-produced a "BBC My World" program series to explain the story behind news and provide teens with information about addressing fake news.

Social networking services

Another type of communication channel has a different premise: to serve as a conduit for its users to share information. This kind of channel, a social network, existed before the Internet, such as amateur radio or even the village square. However, the Internet has facilitated an explosion of social networking services. While online community services fall under the umbrella of social networking, they are usually group or interest-centered, such as discussion boards, chat rooms and user forums. Usually such virtual communities have an identified purpose and group norms for interacting; even amateur radio operators require a license, and the license owner is responsible for its operations. On the other hand, social networking services tend to be individual-centered, with the intent that each person can contact others and share information with them: one-to-one or one-to-many. Such communication channels generally do not create, select or curate information; in fact, many services explicitly state that they are not responsible for the information conveyed via the channel, including fake news. Facebook is the most widely known example, now with more than a billion and a half users (20 percent of the world's population). Other popular social networking services include Instagram, Twitter, QQ, WhatsApp, WeChat, Tumblr, QZone, Baidu Tieba, Sina Weibo, YY, Snapchat and VKontakte. Other social networking services have specific niches such as LinkedIn for professional networking, ResearchGate for scholarly discussion, Fishbrain for fishing, and English, baby! for language learning.

Social networking services enable people to create profiles, "friends" lists, and postings of text and usually other media. Their information may be shared with just a few individuals or open to all public users. In addition, nothing stops users from employing bots to generate messages such as fake news. Most social networking services do not require a subscription fee, although some charge for premium access and contributing. Instead, they tend to sell advertising space or sell their user lists to marketers. With this business model, preferences may be given to paid "customers," which may include creators of fake news.

Not surprisingly, Facebook shares more fake news than mainstream media outlets, not only because of the ease of spreading the news and the huge user base, but also because there is less effort or responsibility to ensure accurate news. In researching influential social media services, Abramson (2019) found that Facebook thought that their users should be the ones to discern the validity of content; it was not the responsibility of the social media service. Indeed, some social networking sites, such as YouTube, pay video creators money for attracting large viewing audiences, which can incentivize those creators to make fake news videos, which further exacerbates the problem. Because of the proliferation of fake news on social networking service websites, as well as trolling and cyberbullying, these services are coming under greater scrutiny (Allcott & Gentzkow, 2017).

Some social networking services are trying self-regulating strategies to curtail fake news. As a proactive measure, some social networking services are cracking down on accounts, requiring real-name policies. Other social networking services are employing fact-checkers or outsourcing fact-checking to verify postings' accuracy, although such efforts are labor- and time-consuming. Although technically not a media outlet, Google's News Initiative is a founding partner of Fire Draft, a website that provides guidance on finding and verifying content from social media. Other services include fact-checking bots as front-line determinators of fake news, but these tools too can reflect the bias of their developers and are not transparent. As a step further and a way to pass on fact-checking costs to their users, some social networking services are considering "premium" services that would exclude advertisements and apparent fake news (Andorfer, 2017). As an alternative strategy, some social networking services are testing the effectiveness of tagging misleading information as "disputed" or "rated false." In experimenting with such tagging efforts, Clayton et al. (2019) found that giving a general warning about misleading information was more effective than tagging an article headline. Such well-intentioned efforts have limited impact. For instance, Facebook removed less than 30 percent of illegal content within a day, and Twitter also removed less than 30 percent. The posting and sharing of fake news are so quick and viral that it is hard to control, especially when users distrust traditional media (Niklewicz, 2017).

Government agencies

Self-imposed restrictions have a checkered history in parts of the media sector, so legal measures may need to be deployed to address fake news. For instance, Article 10 of the 1950 convention for the Protection of Human Rights and Fundamental Freedom stated that everyone has the right to freedom of expression, but it also stated that the exercise of this freedom also incurs responsibilities, and may be restricted in order to protect the rights or reputations of others (Richter, 2019). Even the United States First Amendment has its limits, and freedom of the press is still accountable to the law. The most common concern is defamation of character: labeled as slander if unrecorded, and as libel if recorded. Another legal tort is intentional infliction of emotional distress. In both cases, the burden is on the defamed party, which is harder to prove for public figures. Fake news creators sometimes copy text or visual content, and give it a false slant, without the originators' permission; likewise, such creators may disguise their website to make it look like an existing media outlet's webpage (e.g., ABCnews.com.co). These actions constitute intellectual property violation, so it can be contested in court as well (Klein & Wueller, 2017). Fake news is more likely to attack marginalized groups such as immigrants, but group defamation is harder to prove than individual libel, especially since fake news often includes a modicum of truth. These victimized groups are also less likely to have the voice or power to correct misleading statements or to sue (Grambo, 2019).

In the United States, traditional media outlets are generally regulated by the Federal Communications Commission (FCC); in 2015 the FCC reclassified broadband Internet access as a telecommunications service so such Internet service providers are also regulated to some extent. The commission oversees licensing, broadband access, media responsibility and public safety. For instance, the FCC can revoke a radio or television station's license if it does not meet the public interest, convenience or necessity. Media stations are also accountable for any indecency or obscenity broadcast. Nevertheless, federal regulations have their limitations. For instance, their legal framework for political advertisements is insufficient in terms of addressing disclaimers, disclosure and foreign influence. Especially with digital communication, even intellectual property law lags behind practice (Wood & Ravel, 2018). The 1962 European Convention on the International Right of Correction stated that false or distorted news should be corrected, but that regulation has rarely been enforced (Richter, 2019). The European Union's (EU) 2010 Directive on Audiovisual Media Services focuses on the right of anyone to reply to incorrect facts in television programs, and the EU Council contends that this approach is appropriate for online media, although their recommendation is non-binding.

Legislators in some countries are trying to regulate social networking services in the same way as other commercial speech disseminated by mainstream media outlets. As neutral conduits or intermediaries of user-generated content, social networking services have tended to be protected under the United States Communications Decency Act of 1996, and the European Parliament has a similar view about the liability of Internet intermediaries. Niklewicz (2017) contended that social networking services can no longer be considered merely as Internet intermediaries because those companies tend to evaluate, filter and prioritize certain content, which constitute editorial processes. Taking a positive approach, the European Commission presented a report in 2018 titled "Tackling Online Disinformation," which encouraged transparency and high-quality information (Richter, 2019).

Another proposed solution from Europe, "Correct the Record," would require social networking services to direct users who see fake news to be presented with fact-check notifications (Perrigo, 2019). Germany proposed demanding that social networking services delete blatant false information within a limited time period or face fines. Niklewicz (2017) proposed a process that starts with the affected party of fake news. That person or group would notify the social networking service, who then would need to do one of the following actions: fact-check the content and decide what next action to take, delete the item, ask the author to delete it (or else it would be automatically deleted), or do nothing and face possible legal consequences. Alternatively, the service could refer the posted content to an independent court, as is done in the European Union for newspaper content.

At the same time, such law makers also need to consider the open market for real news and free speech rights (Andorfer, 2017). The Organization for Security and Co-operation in Europe supports media self-regulation principles and mechanisms to preserve freedom of speech (Richter, 2019). Interestingly, people who share a partisan identity and external political efficacy tend to think that fake news impacts outsiders more than their own insider groups; therefore, they recommend media literacy efforts rather than media regulation because they do not want their own access to social media reduced (Jang & Kim, 2018).

Notwithstanding the intent to curtail fake news, government agencies themselves need to be regulated just like all the other stakeholders. In reviewing fake news in light of the United States' First Amendment and other existing legislation, Calvert et al. (2018) concluded that

> private efforts to combat fake news, including counterspeech, self-regulation and media literacy education, are far superior to creating a government agency vested with Orwellian authority to determine what news is true and false and, in turn, to censor the latter.
>
> *(p. 107)*

Consumers and knowledge

In the final analysis, fake news is a human endeavor. Few individuals would create fake news if no one read it. Individuals might knowingly read fake news for entertainment or even as a test to see if they can identify it. Others might believe fake news because it confirms their own convictions, even when faced with facts to the contrary. However, those people who truly cannot distinguish between real and fake news are the most at risk because they may make decisions that have dire consequences such as dying from dangerous diets. When such negative effects result, those same people may feel victimized and assert: "I didn't know. I didn't realize it was fake news." Yet they may find it hard to win a legal suit, particularly in light of the disclaimers that the media sector include.

The underlying factor is knowledge: of oneself and of the external world. The first addresses the idea of an open and independent mind set – even when cognizant of personal biases. Such self-knowledge comes from reflection on how one reacts to the external world. Over time, individuals generalize from their experiences so they can apply their learning to novel situations. For instance, rather than treating each human encounter as a totally new experience, people learn how to predict patterns of interaction, say between encountering a bus driver on the way to work as opposed to a person with a gun in a dark alley. Individuals' experiences start from familial beliefs that are absorbed subconsciously to become cultural biases to life-changing events such as bankruptcy or divorce that lead to cognitive biases (Baeza-Yates, 2018). Those same patterns and biases occur relative to individuals' encounter with news. For instance, anger tends to encourage partisan assessment that reinforces current beliefs while anxiety tends to look for more factual information (Weeks, 2015), so individuals can identify their own emotional triggers that could distort their interpretations of fake news. Bias is also more likely to occur when individuals experience information overload; they give limited attention to each news story and, instead, go for emotional headlines or depend on their friends to curate the news (Ciampaglia & Menczer, 2018). Fortunately, studies (e.g., Nelson, 2013) have also found that when individuals are confronted with their own biases, they become less biased unconsciously. For that reason, the more that one understands psychology, including peer pressure and manipulation, the more self-aware one can become, and can self-regulate personal reactions to news. Ironically, though, such self-recognition and self-regulation usually require learning from others. Whom do you trust? What is the evidence?

As people engage with their external world, they are likely to experience it in relation to their interaction with other humans. People are social animals, and are influenced by others for several reasons; they may think others know better, they want to belong and be accepted by others, or they fear for their own safety if they disagree with others in power. The crux of the matter is assessing information based on the evidence rather than the impact of another person (Spinney, 2017). Another stumbling block to an open disposition is the perception that the first impression is the correct one, as reflected in the saying: "Don't confuse me with facts; my mind is made up." For some people, changing one's mind shows weakness or lack of principle, and compromises one's integrity. Again, such an attitude reveals a need for social affirmation rather than self-reliance. Changing one's mind can be difficult, as can be any change in general. People tend to prefer the known status quo rather than the unknown. The new information has to be more compelling and beneficial than the old information because it takes psychological and mental energy to go from equilibrium to disequilibrium; the new equilibrium has to be worth that cost. Fake news leverages these human attitudes. Getting the fake news out quickly, especially before the real news appears or before people can discuss it with their colleagues, gives that fake news a psychological edge and more credence. Secondly, fake news travels faster and is shared by peers more than real news, so the social benefits of believing fake news outweigh holding off evaluation until all the news arrives. Especially in the face of the flood of news, it is easier to go along with what friends believe. The psychological cost, though, is giving up one's own control (Van Dijk, 2006). In that respect, knowledge about sociology can help individuals become more aware of social pressures and determine the validity of those social pressures, including those expressed in fake news.

Because knowledge of the external world depends on learning from direct experience and learning from others' experiences, parents and guardians serve as the first teachers to help youngsters discern what is true and what is false, especially as children see parents' feelings. Issues such as the COVID-19 pandemic illustrate the need for family discussions about accurate information and sources. Parents and guardians can also model ethical digital use (Livingstone, 2020).

That need for a strong knowledge base to determine the veracity of news and other information constitutes one of the main reasons for formal education: to efficiently and equitably prepare people to survive and succeed in daily life rather than learn completely from trial and error or to depend completely on other people. Learning about social studies and the sciences gives people content knowledge against which to test new information. Language arts helps people learn how to understand, interpret and generate communication in different formats. Learning in groups helps individuals learn social skills. In short, education helps people become literate and gain knowledge for themselves. This knowledge then helps them to discern and address fake news.

Educators and information professionals

To facilitate how to learn thus places responsibility on educators and other information professionals such as librarians. It is easy to think that literacy in itself will solve the problem of fake news. Some people find it difficult to transfer knowledge and processes from one domain to another, or from one situation to another. Just as some people need to be taught explicitly about good manners or how to take notes, people may need explicit training on how to distinguish real news from fake news. It is inevitable that people will encounter fake news so having the tools to recognize such disinformation is a useful life skill.

Surprisingly, then, traditional K–12 curriculum seldom included news media explicitly. One of the main reasons for such omission is that traditional media outlets and information organizations such as libraries were expected to evaluate, vet and monitor information before it was disseminated. Even today, school textbooks are thoroughly reviewed before being adopted by state and local educational institutions, and they often constitute the main source of information in some courses. Likewise, libraries have selection policies and carefully select materials for their permanent collections. Individuals just needed to know if the information was understandable and relevant.

The open nature of the Internet, especially with the expansion of social media and social networking services, shortcuts those evaluative and monitoring processes. Each individual has to evaluate the quality of information personally. Increasingly, librarians are teaching users how to evaluate information, particularly websites, drawing upon their own professional training as information professionals. Likewise, formal educational institutions are recognizing the need for media literacy instruction, including news literacy, from grade school to adult education. For instance, in studying how college students engage with news, Head et al. (2018) reported that:

> The interplay between unmediated and mediated pathways to news underscored the value of the socialness of news; discussions with peers, parents, and professors helped students identify which stories they might follow and trust. Opportunities and strategies are identified for preparing students to gather and evaluate credible news sources, first as students and then as lifelong learners.
>
> (p. 1)

Curricular efforts to include news literacy are occurring from local schools to international organizations such as UNESCO. In the United States, curriculum decisions are generally made at the local and state levels, so the inclusion of news literacy is uneven. The 2019 National Association for Media Literacy education report on media literacy education in the U.S. stated that the main media literacy topics were information literacy and news literacy, and about a third of the instruction occurred in stand-alone courses. As an example, in 2018, California's legislators passed Senate Bill 830: "To ensure that young adults are prepared with media literacy skills necessary to safely, responsibly, and critically consume and use social media and other forms of media," which explicitly mentioned fabricated news stories. Yet even this bill only mandated a list of media literacy resources to support media literacy in the classroom, not a mandate to actually instruct or develop a curriculum. Even widely adopted United States Common Core State Standards, which assert that learners should gather data from multiple sources and assess their credibility and accuracy, do not explicitly mention news literacy. Media and information literacy has greater agency in Europe. For example, in 2013 UNESCO developed a media and information literacy assessment framework, which informed Sweden's commission to develop a national agenda for media and an information literate citizenry. By 2018 Sweden's Schools Inspectorate (Skolinspektionen) required the integration of media literacy and source evaluation in the national curriculum (Carlsson, 2019), which also noted the role of school librarians to teach that skill. Finland is another country that is addressing fake news through education and government response (Peters et al., 2018). News literacy and relevant curriculum are detailed later in this book.

Of course, to be effective instructors, educators themselves need to be news literate. In general, such skills can be presumed. However, even educators can be fooled by digital image manipulation; their default stance is to compare images to text, and spot possible discrepancies. They can also draw upon their subject expertise and common sense to ascertain the probability of the fake news content, such as Bill Gates buying the Vatican. However, educators would do well to hone their photo-editing skills or try out fact-checking and source-training tools, which they can then share with their students. For example, UNESCO created a media and information literacy curriculum for teachers (Wilson et al., 2011). Nevertheless, such instruction for pre- and in-service teacher programs is uneven at best; even teachers and journalism educators need to ramp up their news literacy skills in this age of social media and expanded fake news (Muratova & Grizzle, 2019). Fortunately, as media literate information professionals, librarians are available to update educators so the potential for professional development is certainly ready for implementation. In addition, librarians can show how news literacy spans the curriculum, and can connect the school community with outside experts and journalists.

It is time for everyone to take responsibility.

References

Abramson, J. (2019). *Merchants of truth: The business of news and the fight for facts.* New York, NY: Simon & Schuster.

Allcott, H., & Gentzkow, M. (2017). Social media and fake news in the 2016 election. *Journal of Economic Perspectives, 31*(2), 211–236.

Andorfer, A. (2017). Spreading like wildfire: Solutions for abating the fake news problem on social media via technology controls and government regulation. *Hastings Law Journal*, *69*(5), 1409–1431.

Baeza-Yates, R. (2018). Bias on the Web. *Communications of the ACM*, *61*(6), 54–61.

Bennett, W. (2008). Changing citizenship in the digital age. In W. Bennett (Ed.), *Civic life online: Learning how digital media can engage youth* (pp. 1–24). Cambridge, MA: The MIT Press.

Berinsky, A. (2015). Rumors and health care reform: Experiments in political misinformation. *British Journal of Political Science*. doi: 10.1017/S0007123415000186.

Bobkowski, P., & Younger, K. (2019). *Be credible: Information literacy for journalism, public relations, advertising and marketing students* (2nd ed.). Lawrence, KS: University of Kansas.

California State Senate. (2018). *Senate Bill No. 830 Pupil instruction: Media literacy: Resources*. Sacramento, CA: California State Senate.

Calvert, C., McNeff, S., Vining, A., & Zarate, S. (2018). Fake news and the First Amendment: Reconciling a disconnect between theory and doctrine. *University of Cincinnati Law Review*, *86*(3), 99–138.

Carlson, M. (2009). The reality of a fake image: News norms, photojournalistic craft, and Brian Walski's fabricated photograph. *Journalism Practice*, *3*(2), 125–139.

Carlsson, U. (Ed.). (2019). *Understanding media and information literacy (MIL) in the digital age*. Gothenburg, Sweden: UNESCO.

Ciampaglia, G., & Menczer, F. (2018, June 21). Biases make people vulnerable to misinformation spread by social media. *Scientific American*. www.scientificamerican.com/article/biases-make-people-vulnerable-to-misinformation-spread-by-social-media/

Clayton, K., Blair, S., Busam, J. A., Forstner, S., Glance, J., Green, G., … & Sandhu, M. (2019). Real solutions for fake news? Measuring the effectiveness of general warnings and fact-check tags in reducing belief in false stories on social media. *Political Behavior*, 1–23.

Coppins, M. (2020). The 2020 disinformation war. *Atlantic*, *325*(2), 28–39.

Frechette, J. (2016). From print newspapers to social media: News literacy in a networked environment. *Studies*, *9*(40), 545–560.

Gibney, E. (2017, October 6). The scientist who spots fake videos. *Nature News*. https://doi.org/10.1038/nature.2017.22784

Goodman, R., & Steyn, E. (Eds.). (2017). *Global journalism education in the 21st century: Challenges & innovations*. Austin, TX: University of Texas.

Grambo, K. (2019). Fake news and racial, ethnic, and religious minorities: A precarious quest for truth. *Journal of Constitutional Law*, *21*(5), 1299–1348.

Haider, J., & Sundin, O. (2019). How do you trust? In U. Carlsson (Ed.), *Understanding media and information literacy (MIL) in the digital age: A question of democracy* (pp. 107–112). Gothenburg, Sweden: University of Gothenburg.

Haigh, M., Haigh, T., & Kozak, N. I. (2018). Stopping fake news: The work practices of peer-to-peer counter propaganda. *Journalism Studies*, *19*(14), 2062–2087.

Head, A., Wihbey, J., Metaxas, P., MacMillan, M., & Cohen, D. (2018). *How students engage with news: Five takeaways for educators, journalists, and librarians*. Chicago, IL: Association of College and Research Libraries.

Hobbs, R. (2016). Literacy: Understanding media and how they work. *What Society Needs from Media in the Age of Digital Communication*, *21*, 131–160.

Hutt, D. (2017, May 9). Fake news, real danger in Southeast Asia. *Asia Times*, 9.

Ireton, C., & Posetti, J. (2018). *Journalism, "fake news" & disinformation*. Paris: UNESCO.

Jang, S. M., & Kim, J. K. (2018). Third person effects of fake news: Fake news regulation and media literacy interventions. *Computers in Human Behavior*, *80*, 295–302.

Keiser, B. (2019). Fragmented truths: Who's doing what to minimize fake. *Online Searcher*, *43*(6), 10–17.

Khaldarova, I., & Pantti, M. (2016). Fake news: The narrative battle over the Ukrainian conflict. *Journalism Practice, 10*(7), 891–901.

Klein, D., & Wueller, J. (2017). Fake news: A legal perspective. *Journal of Internet Law, 20*(10), 1–13.

Livingstone, S. (2020, April 1). Coronavirus and #fakenews: What should families do? *Parenting for a Digital Future*, 1–5.

Messaris, P., & Abraham, L. (2001). The role of images in framing news stories. In S. Reese, O. Gandy, Jr., & A. Grant (Eds.), *Framing public life* (pp. 231–242). New York, NY: Routledge.

Mitchell, A., Gottfried, J., Stocking, G., Walker, M., & Fedeli, S. (2019). *Many Americans say made-up news is a critical problem that needs to be fixed*. Washington, DC: Pew Research Center.

Muratova, N., & Grizzle, A. (2019). *Media and information literacy in journalism: A handbook for journalists and journalism educators*. Tashkent, Uzbekistan: Baktria Press.

National Association for Media Literacy Education. *Snapshot 2019: The state of media literacy education in the U.S.* New York, NY: National Association for Media Literacy Education.

National Press Photographers Association. (2019). *Code of ethics*. Athens, GA: National Press Photographers Association. https://nppa.org/code-ethics

Nelson, M. (2013). The hidden persuaders: Then and now. *Journal of Advertising, 37*(1), 113–126.

Newman, N., Fletcher, R., Kalogeropoulos, A., Levy, D., & Nielsen, R. K. (2017). *Reuters Institute digital news report 2017*. Oxford, UK: Reuters Institute.

Ngumbi, E. (2019, February 21). Scientists need to talk to the public. *Scientific American*. https://blogs.scientificamerican.com/observations/scientists-need-to-talk-to-the-public/

Niklewicz, K. (2017). *Weeding out fake news: An approach to social media regulation*. Brussels, Belgium: Wilfried Martens Centre for European Studies.

Ortiz, D. (2018, November 14). Could this be the cure for fake news? *BBC Future*. www.bbc.com/future/article/20181114-could-this-game-be-a-vaccine-against-fake-news

Perrigo, B. (2019, February 28). How this radical new proposal could curb fake news on social media. *Time*. https://time.com/5540995/correct-the-record-polling-fake-news/

Peters, A., Tartari, E., Lotfinejad, N., Parneix, P., & Pittet, D. (2018). Fighting the good fight: the fallout of fake news in infection prevention and why context matters. *Journal of Hospital Infection, 100*(4), 365–370.

Richter, A. (2019). Accountability and media literacy mechanisms as a counteraction to disinformation in Europe. *Journal of Digital Media & Policy, 10*(3), 311–327.

Rusbridger, A. (2018). *Breaking news: The remaking of journalism and why it matters now*. Edinburgh, Scotland: Canongate.

Samuel, A. (2016, November 29). To fix fake news, look to yellow journalism. *Jstor Daily*. https://daily.jstor.org/to-fix-fake-news-look-to-yellow-journalism/

Schiffrin, A., Santa-Wood, B., & De Martino, S. (2019). *Bridging the gap: Rebuilding citizen trust in media*. Washington, DC: Open Society Foundations.

Skolinspektionen. (2018) *Undervisning om källkritiskt förhållningssätt. [Schools Inspectorate. Teaching on source critique approach]*. Stockholm, Sweden: Skolinspektionen.

Society of Professional Journalists. (2014). *Code of ethics*. Indianapolis, IN: Society of Professional Journalists.

Spinney, L. (2017). How Facebook, fake news and friends are warping your memory. *Nature News, 543*(7644), 168.

Stakston, B. (2019). Real case journalism and media literacy in schools. In U. Carlsson (Ed.), *Understanding media and information literacy (MIL) in the digital age: A question of democracy* (pp. 219–224). Gothenburg, Sweden: University of Gothenburg.

Toggle, C. A. (1998). The bias toward finding bias in television news. *Communication Reports, 11*(1), 65–72.

UNESCO. (2013). *Global media and information literacy assessment framework: Country readiness and competencies.* Paris: UNESCO.

Van Dijk, T. A. (2006). Discourse and manipulation. *Discourse & Society, 17*(3), 359–383.

Weeks, B. (2015). Emotions, partisanship, and misperceptions: How anger and anxiety moderate the effect of partisan bias on susceptibility to political misinformation. *Journal of Communication, 65*(4), 699–719.

Wilson, C., Grizzle, A., Tuazon, R., Akyempong, K., & Cheung, C. K. (2011). *Media and information literacy curriculum for teachers.* Paris: UNESCO.

Wood, A., & Ravel, A. (2018). Fool me once: Regulating fake news and other online advertising. *Southern California Law Review, 91*(6), 1223–1278.

5
THE LITERACY CONTEXT

Generically, literacy refers to abilities to comprehend, evaluate, use and generate. The ability to discern fake news is considered a subset of news literacy, which falls under the context of media (as in mass media) literacy, which, in turn, is part of information literacy. Information literacy is the ability to locate, access, select, evaluate, manage, use, create and communicate information effectively and responsibly. Fake news also requires language literacy of functional reading and writing, digital literacy, visual literacy and numeracy/data literacy. The following diagram (Figure 5.1) provides a visual conceptualization of the relationships among literacies. Note that some of the literacies extend a bit beyond information literacy, largely because of mechanical or visceral aspects.

For the purposes of addressing fake news, basic language literacy is assumed, largely because in the discussion about news literacy, issues of linguistic text are covered. For each of the other literacies, this chapter discusses how creators employ literacies to produce news literacy, and how the different forms of literacy inform the discernment of fake news. Each literacy section provides a sample of related learning activities to gain competencies in the specific literacy as it applies to discerning fake news and other information.

News literacy

The most specific literacy associated with fake news is news literacy. News is produced by media outlets, both mainstream and alternative sources. At its most basic level, news literacy involves accessing, selecting, understanding, evaluating, interpreting, organizing and communicating news messages in a variety of formats. Maksl, Ashley and Craft (2015) drew upon Potter's (2010) five basic knowledge structures for media literacy – knowledge about media content, media industries,

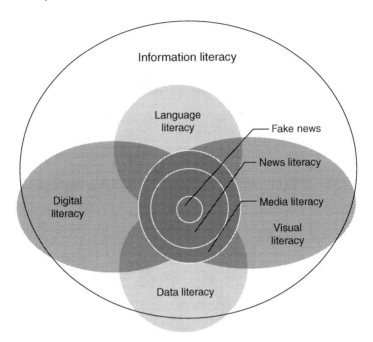

FIGURE 5.1 Conceptual relationships among literacies

media effects, the real world and the self – to provide a framework to assess one's level of news literacy. These elements also reflect journalists' knowledge base. To that end, this discussion will pose the concept of thinking like a journalist using the communication cycle as a mental framework.

News information neighborhoods

First, what is the information that journalists seek? Maksl, Ashley and Craft (2015) identified five information "neighborhoods" that journalists are likely to encounter.

- Raw information. Nowadays, almost all people can express themselves digitally as well as in print and orally. Such information is typically unfiltered and unedited, reflecting a spectrum of quality. By definition, raw information is unverified, and the poster is not held accountable for the way that the information is used.
- Propaganda. Political operatives and other organizations produce subjective arguments with emotional manipulation to build mass support for action, some of which may be ideological in nature. Propagandists do not feel accountable to correct possible errors that they might make; journalists, on the other hand, need to verify propaganda and should reveal the context and counterpoints to the propaganda.

- Publicity. Spokespersons and publicists promote people and events through various communication means, giving a positive view. Sometimes the publicist pays to have the information disseminated. They will also usually correct any errors to prevent any backlash publicity. Journalists try to avoid any conflict of interest such as remuneration or special favors when covering the person or event. Closely related to publicity is advertising, which is in the business of selling goods and services. Journalists themselves usually do not deal with advertisements; the media outlet should mark "sponsored" information as advertisements.
- Entertainment. To engage and amuse people is the goal of performers, artists, writers and producers. They are accountable for their work, and may correct errors. Journalists may entertain, but their chief goal is accurate information; they may, however, cover and critique entertainment events.
- News. As noted above, news consists of the reporting of timely natural and human-made events that interest and impact the public. The chief goal is to inform, although news can be entertaining and can publicize. Journalists are accountable for their work; they are supposed to verify information and correct errors as promptly as possible.

To be news literate, people need to be able to distinguish among these information neighborhoods, and weigh their relative value. Each kind of information serves a role, so individuals do not have to ignore these different kinds of information, but they need to realize each one's objective and means, just as journalists do. In other words, news literate people control their response to information, not be controlled by it.

Journalists are in the business of gathering and reporting news, not creating it, although the information they find may result in being newsworthy, such as uncovering a secret impactful plan. In any case, journalists need to be good observers and networkers to identify potential and occurring news. Furthermore, they need to seek the source of the information, and validate the information and the sources. Is it true and relevant? So too should news literate consumers. Just like everyone else, journalists can be overloaded with information, shifting through it to determine if it is newsworthy or not (e.g., "A dog biting a man is not newsworthy, but a man biting a dog is"). For that reason, many news organizations employ several journalists, each with her or his own "beat" (i.e., community or subject area). Journalists not only recognize newsworthy information, but they seek reputable news sources, such as government officials, organizational leaders, and subject experts. They too use fact-checking tools, research the authority of sources, analyze data and statistics, track existing source materials, and collect background information. In the process, journalists try to distinguish between assertion versus verification and between evidence versus inference (Kovach & Rosenstiel, 2010). In counterpart, news literate consumers seek out the sources of information as mentioned in news items. Journalists have a responsibility to quote and restate information accurately within the original context. As news literate consumers recognize the reporting of journalists and news organizations, they too can rely on those news sources that are reputable.

As noted above, journalists need to verify information. Is the information reliable? Even if their source has provided accurate information as a rule, journalists try to get a confirmation of that information from another source as well, be it through direct observation, an independent person, or a relevant document. Journalists then triangulate the information to confirm reliability – or to uncover inconsistencies that need further investigation. So too should news literate consumers check news items, especially if those items are particularly significant or surprising to the consumer, with other sources of the same event or asserted fact.

Processing news information

News inconsistencies or variations are to be expected in that different people perceive an event or situation uniquely because of their experiences, knowledge base or attitudes. No two people even experience a speech or a place in exactly the same way. A restaurant opening, for instance, impacts a family, a neighborhood property owner, a traffic cop, a grocer, another restaurant owner, a nearby shop owner, a tax collector and a government official in unique ways. If that restaurant burns down, it again affects each previously mentioned stakeholder – as well as additional ones such as firefighters and insurance claims adjusters – differently. A journalist should provide the basic facts that all of these people could agree upon, such as place and time, but may also detail how each stakeholder might experience the event and how it affects them. Furthermore, each stakeholder might have a different agenda in connecting with a journalist, such as promoting or disparaging the event or person, seeking self-importance, or advancing their own agenda. In other cases, the informant may have misunderstood or misinterpreted information – or may have simply lied. Verifying information can be a complex process as journalists try to ferret out the truth. Moreover, different journalists might interview different people, or prioritize different aspects of the same story. Therefore, news literate consumers should realize the possible variations on a news story, and may want to pursue some of those different types of coverage, especially if the angle is particularly relevant to that consumer.

These different perspectives inform journalists' interpretation and analysis of the news story. Journalists have a unique relationship with, and responsibility to, their consumers; they "explain what public events mean and what audiences can do to prepare for what will happen next, and competently convey information that is accessible to the audience" (Muratova & Grizzle, 2019, p. 32). As noted elsewhere, a variety of news stories may be written: straight news reporting of facts discovered by the journalist or presented to him or her, analysis of the news story, or an opinion piece (Otero, 2017). The greater the extent of analysis, the more that journalists have to justify their stance through compelling and convincing evidence, confirmation by other experts, and relevant context. A thorough analysis also calls for a fair and balanced perspective; opposing viewpoints and possibly conflicting evidence need to be incorporated so that a variety of factors can be considered and weighed before a judgment can be pronounced. Journalists also need to recognize their own perspectives and biases as they investigate the different sides of a complex news story. To that end, they need to lay out the facts, and make conclusions that may be uncomfortable with their own values in the service of accuracy and truth. Thus, analysis requires more time, investigation, verification, and a resultant longer exposure. News literate consumers should likewise keep an open mind as they seek the truth behind the news and develop new and more informed understanding.

Time is a crucial factor in gathering and analyzing information as a news literate person, be it a journalist or news consumer. Hardly ever does anyone have all the facts in a news story; it is difficult to gather and understand the entire background and context of the story, including all the people involved. One critical feature of news is its timeliness, so journalists often have to report the information as they see it and can collect available, reputable sources quickly. With the Internet, and especially social media, that timeframe is even more compressed. The fact that social media posters do not have to have their news vetted by editors or other overseers means that their news, including fake news, can be published more quickly than a news organization's journalist report. Journalists are more likely to follow up on a breaking news story with additional details, context and background information. Hopefully, those added features will also be considered news as new information is revealed, but in some cases such follow-up information might not get the publicity of the original story. News literate consumers are in the same situation, not knowing all the facts before accessing a news story. It behooves consumers to remember the time and effort it takes to get the facts, all of the facts. Consumers should not jump on the first news blast but, instead, wait for reputable news sources to gain more complete, verified information whenever possible.

Lastly, journalists communicate the news, regardless of the type or depth of coverage, in an accurate, clear, fair and transparent manner. Particularly in straight fact reporting, journalists should avoid highly emotional language, editorial comments or irrelevant details: "Just the facts, ma'am." Even in-depth analysis and opinion pieces should avoid rousing terms or hyperbole. News literate consumers should be sensitive to such emotionally-charged statements, and self-examine their own emotional triggers that might influence their responses. It should be noted that sometimes a different person than the reporter writes the news story's headline, which might use more eye-catching phrases. Similarly, pull-quotes taken out of context might veer from the story's heart. Additionally, images might accompany the story, which might not be under the journalist's control both in terms of what the image captures or how it is edited; in fact, an image could misconstrue or mislead the consumer. For that reason, news literate consumers should give less credence to headlines than to the full story's information itself, and certainly should not share a story until they have examined it completely. Even then, it is good practice for sharers to explicitly state their own stance relative to the news story's quality and perspective so that their own audience interprets the story in light of the sharers' mindset.

News literacy activities

The following list offers substantive projects to help learners gain and practice news literacy.

- The *New York Times'* teaching and learning site (www.nytimes.com/section/learning) offers lesson plans on almost any subject, and their news and information topics are great, such as this lesson on spotting fake news: www.nytimes.com/2017/01/19/learning/lesson-plans/evaluating-sources-in-a-post-truth-world-ideas-for-teaching-and-learning-about-fake-news.html
- News in Education Online works with newspapers to provide weekly classroom resources on news literacy: https://nieonline.com
- PBS offers lesson plans that coincide with PBS Newshour: www.pbs.org/newshour/extra/lessons-plans/lesson-plan-how-to-teach-your-students-about-fake-news/
- The News Literacy Project and the E.W. Scripps Company co-developed National News Literacy Week (end of January) to raise awareness of news literacy: https://newslit.org/news-literacy-week/. The News Literacy Project also offers news literacy lessons via their product Checkology: https://newslit.org/educators/checkology/
- Stony Brook University Center for News Literacy has news literacy lessons: https://digitalresource.center/lets-get-started

Visual literacy

Visual literacy includes one's ability to comprehend, interpret and produce visual information (such as images). Visual literacy predates textual literacy, and is re-emerging as an important literacy, especially across a global digital society. Furthermore, technology has enabled images that are presupposed to be accurate, such as photographs, to be manipulated for fake news purposes. It should be noted that, while principles of visual "language" are universal, their meanings may be culturally defined or depend on the image's context. Fake images can leverage those universal and contextual connotations to mislead viewers. Especially with today's sophisticated digital tools, audiences need to be visually literate to a new degree.

Visual representations

Visual representations may be considered in terms of their form and their function. For example, a sign is a one-to-one correspondence between two objects, such as a drawing of a ship and the ship itself. The more that one wants to particularize the original, the more detail or resemblance, verisimilitude, is required. The payoff is that little interpersonal coding is needed to understand what the signified object is. A visual representation may also serve as a symbol: a codified representation that stands for something else, such as a flag symbolizes a nation. A symbol does not have to be realistic; its strength is in its associative or connotative meaning. However, the more abstract or arbitrary, the greater the need for the social act of codification. For instance, a feather might represent a bird, flight or cowardice (which has a distinctive cultural connotation). As the example demonstrates, visual representations are influenced by the relationship they have with the viewer, and reflect cultural beliefs and norms as much as they reflect the intended information itself and its medium (Morra & Smith, 2006).

Visual journalists

In terms of news, a case could be made that visuals predate writing as early humans recorded news about their hunts on cave walls using stone instruments. Paintings heralded significant events such as political appointments and battles. Finally, photographs could capture news in real time, such as casualties in the Mexican-American War: the first war to be photographed. These latter images brought a new realism to visual messages, and within ten years photography techniques had advanced to the degree that Civil War photos could be mass-produced and disseminated (Gervais, 2010). In the 19th century, when newspapers blossomed, images engraved on wood started appearing in the 1830s – to be largely replaced by photo reproductions before the end of the century. While visual messages exist as drawings, cartoons, charts and icons, this section will focus on photographic visuals. Charts and other data visualization are addressed in the data literacy section.

Reporters used to shoot their own stories, but now visual news is typically gathered by photo and video journalists. Such visual journalists might accompany a reporter or work independently. Likewise, news organizations might hire visual journalists or purchase specific visual news from visual freelancers, either professional or amateur.

Some people trust visual news more than written news because it appears to be more objective and unedited raw information. Visual news highly resembles first-person sensory experience and causes stronger physiological reactions than text (Geise & Baden, 2014). However, just as with any other eyewitness, including traditional reporters, visual journalists select what images they want to capture and what camera techniques they use to record those images. Because they are recording existing visual representations of news, visual journalists could be considered as mediators rather than creators or "authors" of visual messages. On the other hand, an author lends meaning to the object, and it is that meaning-endowed visual that is transmitted. Similarly, the photographer and filmmaker who give contextual meaning to the images they capture may be considered the authors. News consumers should look to see if an image's source is attributed to a person or group; those sources can then be examined for their production history and quality. Unattributed images may signal that they are not to be taken seriously.

These few examples demonstrate the possible complexity of interpreting visual occurrences. Looking through the eyes of a photojournalist serves as a way to gain visual literacy skills. Even if they intend to create a fake visual message (which would contradict journalistic ethical practice), accomplished visual journalists employ visual elements and principles.

Visual elements and principles

Visual professionals generally agree that visual messages are created using seven main elements: line, space, shape, form, value, color and texture. These elements combine to create compositions that reflect principles of art: balance, harmony, rhythm, proportion, emphasis, unity and movement (Webb, 2020). Together, these aspects serve as a visual "grammar" that gives meaning to images. Here are some examples that show how compositions can evoke reactions, which may be manipulated by visual journalists. Understanding this visual grammar helps news consumers recognize how composition infers meaning and separates the art from the information.

- Line. In a composition, lines direct a person's attention. Rays around a person makes them seem more important. Likewise, lines can frame figures, prioritizing them but also limiting them. Horizontal lines may feel more calming while diagonal lines may feel more energetic.
- Space. A lone figure in a large space evokes isolation. A close-up of a face evokes sincerity.
- Shape. Rounded shapes connote softness, comfort, naturalness and possibly weakness. Sharp shapes connote energy, danger and a mechanical sense.
- Form. Form is the three-dimensional shape of an object. A gradual shading of a form makes it appear rounded and perhaps more organic. In contrast, flat forms may seem more austere. Lighting can impact the sense of form; a single source of a focused light can make a form seem starker and less friendly.
- Value. Dark colors can seem foreboding and light colors can feel innocent.
- Color. Warm colors (yellows to reds) can feel more energetic, while cool colors (greens, blues, purples) can feel more peaceful. The intensity of the color attracts attention and can connote an intensity of action.
- Texture. Does a surface look rough? It can connote naturalness, harshness or manliness. A smooth texture can connote calm, richness or femininity. Lighting can emphasize texture, making something seem more tactile – and weather a person's face wrinkles.
- Balance. The distribution of art elements impact balance. A symmetrical image connotes stability. An unbalanced image can connote energy, change or disorder.
- Harmony. Similar shapes and colors make an image more harmonious and comforting.
- Rhythm. Repetition of lines and shapes form a rhythmic pattern, which may be soothing such as gentle waves, or clashing such as plaids against swirls.

- Proportion. People who are out of typical proportion may seem odd. For instance, when a camera lens is very close to a person, it can make that individual look distorted, such as having a large nose. Camera angle can also mislead relative proportion; consider when a person holds out his hand, making it look as if he is holding the Eiffel Tower that is actually far away.
- Emphasis. A photographer can emphasize a part of an image in several ways, typically by leveraging contrasts: centering the main object, having the object take up most of the space, highlighting the object against a darkened background, and directing lines to the important object. Emphasis pushes emotions to the extreme, be they positive or negative.
- Movement. Repetitive and directional lines and shapes give the illusion of movement. Digital camcorders can further manipulate movement by adjusting recording speed. Campaigns can appear growing or stagnant depending on the sense of movement in an image. Movement is also inferred in terms of sequencing images. In fact, traditional film technically consists of a series of still images, which could be reordered when edited. For instance, if images are placed in the wrong order, they can result in misinterpretation, which might be the intent of fake news creators. Such reordered sequencing can even lead to mistrials when images appear to show who attacked first.

Photography itself has several technical elements that result in a photograph: lenses, focus, exposure, depth of field, shutter speed, lighting and film (and its equivalent) (Hedgecoe, 2009). With these elements, visual journalists can create arresting images, sometimes with more focus on esthetic craft than on the information to be recorded (Carlson, 2009). Here are some ways that photojournalists can communicate fake news visually by manipulating these elements and principles. Understanding how images are produced technically helps news consumers realize the possible subjectivity of visual messages.

- Lens. The eye of the camera, the lens, impacts the size, sharpness, perspective and depth of field. If a photographer wants to give a sense of a crowd when in fact few people are present, she can show just the people close to the central figure or event. A wide-angle lens enables a photographer to capture confined spaces close up, which can give the impression of an intimate crowd. An ultra wide-angle lens can also increase the sense of depth and distance; a figure in the back can seem very small, isolated and powerless. A telephoto lens can give a distorted sense of scale. A polarizing lens filter can cut glare, say light bouncing off a person's glasses; seeing a person's eyes can make him look more honest and open.
- Focus. If a photographer wants to make a figure stand out, she can minimize the depth of field so that everything else seems out of focus. In contrast, a maximum depth of field can result in blurring a foreground subject, so that audience reaction can be emphasized instead of the speaker (or it can blur foreground people that would otherwise illustrate a distraction).

- Exposure. Exposure deals with the amount of light needed to record an image. Exposure depends on the camera's aperture (opening) and the shutter speed. A wide aperture leads to a blurred background. A slow shutter speed also blurs action, which can suggest movement and sense of energy. If an image is under-exposed, the figure appears darker and sometimes sinister; over-exposure can make a person look washed-out.
- Lighting. Natural light can be harsh and glaring; if a person is facing the sun, she may need to squint, which might result in an unflattering pose. The time of day impacts the length of a shadow; a long shadow can be ominous – or indicate a long legacy. Shafts of vertical light can connote spirituality. The lighting source can highlight different color tones; a warm tone can be more welcoming and a cool tone can be more austere.

Visual literacy issues

It must be recognized, however, that news-related still and moving images are likely to be edited or even modified before they are disseminated. While the image originator might do the manipulation, news editors and layout directors might crop the visual to fit the space or timeframe of the news publication or broadcast. The choice between a color and a black/white version can also indicate its importance. In either case, the content and inference of the image can change and mislead the viewer. Furthermore, the juxtaposition of the image to the text can have different connotations, at least in terms of relevance. Similarly, the placement of the entire story also indicates its importance; front page news on the upper half of a print newspaper, or the leading story online, is an instant eye-catcher and importance piece. In the final analysis, the media outlet editors have the final say in selecting and deciding the final presentation of visual messages. Therefore, news consumers should also investigate the media outlet's history of image selection or manipulation in terms of their alignment with language commentary, and in terms of their visual connotations detailed above.

Digital visual messages become even more controversial because of sophisticated digital editing tools. News consumers need to advance their visual literacy to digital heights. Art and photographic elements apply well. For instance, inconsistent lighting source and shadows signal image manipulation. Overly smooth areas may be the result of airbrushing. Different-sized pixels and cloned areas indicate editing and sometimes meshing of images. Sometimes image metadata can reveal source codes pointing to efforts to fool the viewer.

Even if the original photojournalist and media outlet do not edit the raw information or mislead the consumer when disseminating visual messages, those same images (especially if in digital format) may be copied and "repurposed" easily by secondary sources who generate and disseminate fake news or misinformation, sometimes without legal permission. For instance, the image might be taken out of context or even completely falsified when applied to a different situation, such as the issue of Pizzagate when photos of restaurant customers and even a photo of

Obama playing ping pong were used as visual evidence of the alleged child sex ring. A recent development is the use of memes to spread fake news, pairing visual and textual popular cultural references to get instant emotional reactions – and sharing. Nowadays with digital images, individuals can edit and modify still and moving images much more easily than with traditional film.

All of these processes are exacerbated when applied to digital video. While single-camera shoots exist, especially in amateur circles or for small events, major media outlets routinely have several cameras shooting from different angles. When events are produced on sets, the director tells the camera crew what shots to take at what angle or distance. Additionally, the sound crew can modify audio effects. Post-production crews can further select and modify the raw material to communicate a specific stance for their target audience. At each step, human bias enters the decision-making, which can mislead the viewer. The same raw footage from a political debate video can be "spun" differently based on which shots are selected, how they are edited, and in what order those shots are sequenced. The classic fictional example is the 1997 film "Wag the Dog," which shows how a war was fabricated using fake video to distract citizens from a presidential scandal. The most recent, sophisticated ploy is deepfake video, which superimposes media, overlaying images and/or sound to misrepresent a person or event, such as literally putting words in another person's mouth or replacing body parts. The advanced technology-enhanced results can be very convincing and, therefore, very troubling especially during political campaigns (Hall, 2018). Visual literacy can help viewers use a critical eye to at least question controversial stances that visual elements enhance or exclude.

Because of these digital manipulations, visually literate news consumers should trace the source of images, and compare the images and their context, such as the verbiage accompanying them, to ascertain their validity. Representative visual fact-checking tools include TinEye, Google Reverse Images, SauceNAO, SurfSafe and RevIMG. Tracking an image source can extend beyond the current image. For instance, images might be "one-offs" of others, such as parodies of the Mona Lisa painting, or they could show the evolution of a commercial brand's history. An interesting recent example is the new U.S. Space Force seal, which provoked much social media comments stating that the seal was a "knock-off" of a Star Trek Starfleet insignia. Tracing back the history of NASA reveals that its original seal could have inspired the Starfleet symbol, so the longer sequencing has a different story line, undercutting the social media recriminations.

One more dimension of visual literacy further impacts the deconstruction of fake images; visual literacy also involves cultural literacy (Wierzbicka, 2005). The term visual anthropology captures these two concepts. People often make meaning of their environment through processes that are culturally defined. Thus, the same image might be interpreted differently by each viewer because of those viewers' cultural world view. Colors, in particular, have different connotations depending on the culture; the color yellow can mean nobility, happiness or cowardness. The acceptable color for a bride's dress may be white, green or red, depending on the culture. Death may be visualized in white or black, depending if you are Western or Eastern. Culture also informs composition norms. For instance, Western images tend to represent faraway objects by making them smaller, while Hindis place distant objects higher on the page but at the same size as close by objects. Focusing at the symbolic level, while some symbols such as a flag, denoting a country or group, is universal, other symbols have culture-specific meaning such as owls, which may be considered wise or evil, for instance. Such cultural norms also exist in moving images; for instance, when given a video recorder to film daily life, Navaho youth portrayed distance and time in ways that do not follow traditional Western filmatic tropes (Worth & Adair, 1972). What fake news images may evoke strong emotions in one culture may just puzzle or be misconstrued in another. Especially as fake news may originate in one culture, and be targeted to another part of the world, misinterpretation or unforeseen consequences may ensue. Visually literate news consumers who realize that the meaning of images have culture-specific connotations, and know culture-specific references, can interpret visual news more accurately and understand the sources of possible visual confusion.

Visual literacy activities

Here are some activities to hone visual literacy skills in discerning fake visual messages in the news.

- The Media Literacy Clearinghouse provides a "Is Seeing Believing" curriculum: http://frankwbaker.com/mlc/is-seeing-believing-curriculum/
- MIT open courseware provides a course with projects, examples and assignments about documentary photography and photojournalism: https://ocw.mit.edu/courses/comparative-media-studies-writing/21w-749-documentary-photography-and-photojournalism-still-images-of-a-world-in-motion-spring-2016/
- New York Times' column "What's going on in this picture?" strips picture captions and asks students to analyze the images: www.nytimes.com/column/learning-whats-going-on-in-this-picture
- The Library of Congress created a five-part video series "Every Photo is a Story" to teach how to analyze photographs, and incorporates exercises for viewers to practice those skills: www.loc.gov/rr/print/coll/fbj/Every_Photo_home.html
- The International Society for Technology in Education's 2012 book Media Literacy in the K-12 Classroom includes a chapter on visual literacy, which guides learners through critical questions and engaging lessons: https://id.iste.org/docs/excerpts/medlit-excerpt.Pdf
- While Mind over Media focuses on propaganda, some of their examples have fake elements, which viewers can evaluate: https://propaganda.mediaeducationlab.com/
- The Museum of Hoaxes includes a hoax photo test to measure the viewer's visual literacy: http://hoaxes.org/tests/hoaxphototest.html. The museum also archives hoax photos, fake viral images and real photos that look fake: http://hoaxes.org/

Audio literacy

Audio literacy is often overlooked because it seems so natural and intuitive as people communicate with sounds from day one. In fact, listening is the first language skill to acquire. Nevertheless, audio literacy comprises several processes with cognitive, affective and behavioral dimensions.

Audio literacy dimensions

As with the other literacies discussed, audio literacy involves the ability to identify, interpret and generate meaningful sounds. Listeners bring their past experiences and knowledge, their linguistic background, other sound (e.g., music) expertise, and their predispositions to the sound situation. Likewise, listeners are influenced by the communication environment and circumstances (Wolvin & Cohen, 2012).

Audio literacy involves several steps, which apply to news (Pearson et al., 2011):

1. Select what to pay attention to: sustain focus for important news.
2. Process information in working memory: interpret and assign meaning to the news.
3. Store and organize information: activate or initiate schema to hold and link news.

Listening to news can involve three types of listening (Pearson et al., 2011):

*   Empathic listening in which listeners try to understand the speakers and their world view.
*   Critical listening in which listeners challenge the speaker's message by evaluating its source, context, accuracy, meaningfulness and use.
*   Active listening, which involves listening carefully, paraphrasing, checking understanding and providing feedback.

Several barriers impact listening, so audio literate persons need to be aware of these barriers and try to mitigate their influence (Pearson et al., 2011).

*   Noise: physical distractions, mental distractions, factual distractions (focus on detail that misses the main point), semantic distractions (over-reacting to emotional words).
*   Perception of others: status (bias because of perceived value of speaker or idea), stereotypes, sights and sound (voice quality affects listening).
*   Self: egocentrism, defensiveness, experiential superiority, personal bias, pseudo-listening (e.g., daydreaming, letting the mind wander).

Producing and disseminating audio messages

As with other literacies, audio literacy entails understanding the processes of generating and disseminating audio messages, including fake news that is broadcast via audio files. Nascent radio held the promise of immediate, authentic news and broad access for the public; as such, audiences often subconsciously trusted the spoken word more than the written word, and they could be more vulnerable to audio fake news than to other media. A classic example of such vulnerability was Orson Welles' radio dramatization of *The War of the Worlds*, which panicked some people even though the show started with a disclaimer about its veracity and intent (Schwartz, 2015). Similar to early television, these radio stations tended to offer a rich variety of programming: news, sports, arts and conversation. Nowadays, real-time radio outlets can rebroadcast news and share audio files with other outlets so that more original news is broadcast, but more duplication of the same news exists (similar to the use of UPI and AP news feeds for newspapers) (Funk, 2017; Lacey, 2013). Because listeners often trust local stations more than national ones, they may be fooled by the news feeds that are downloaded locally, which give the illusion of localness when in actuality the news is more "canned" (Dubber, 2013). On the other hand, online radio can be personalized, based on prior listening choices or conscious personal ratings of shows, to play just what the listener wants to hear – and when. Podcasts are an interesting mix in this respect as some listeners subscribe to, and regularly listen to, podcast series or websites while others search for, and listen to, specific single podcasts (Lacey, 2013). In short, audio outlets can set and carry out their agendas more easily, including the incorporation of fake news, than some other media outlets (Braesel & Karg, 2018).

Radio stations and podcasts may be owned and operated by governments, local community members, non-profit organizations or commercial entities. Compared to television stations, radio stations and podcast channels require less technology, staffing and resources. In addition, they may reflect a wide spectrum of oversight, from rigid selection and censorship to self-determined openness. Similar to television stations, audio outlets can strive to present a variety of content experiences or can narrow-cast them (such as broadcasting only sports news). Radio stations, including options such as ham radio, have been regulated nationally in many countries just as television has been. In the digital age, many more platforms, including podcasts, are available; several of these channels have little regulation (similar to cable TV) or have been de-regulated as happened in New Zealand (Dubber, 2013). Hence, a tension exists between audio news as a public good monitored by the state and free market community-based audio news as a voice of the people. There is room for both, but applying equitable regulations can be challenging. In addition, fake news can emerge in either case.

Currently, 89 percent of Americans 12 years old and older listen to terrestrial radio in a given week, with news as one of the most listened-to radio formats (even though there is generally little news on radio except on public radio and a few all-news commercial radio stations), and a majority of Americans have listened to a podcast (Pew Research Center, 2019a). Furthermore, the number of news podcasts rose globally to almost 12,000 in ten months within the year 2019 (Newman & Gallo, 2019). Typically, radio is listened to more passively, and podcasts tend to engender more listening engagement (Berry, 2016). In some countries, people get their news principally from the radio, and people increasingly listen to podcasts online or downloaded onto their mobile devices. Interestingly, men more than women like to get their news via radio. Podcast listeners tend to be more educated and wealthier as a whole than the average listener, which may reflect the underlying principle of radio as wideband and podcasting as digitally narrowband (Pew Research Center, 2019a). In terms of impact, radio can reach a wide audience to inform quickly with a unified message, which governments can control. Podcasts with their more personal approach foster community through shared stories, and can spark grassroots social change (Dubber, 2013). Again, as a whole, audio outlets can employ fake news to impact their listeners.

What characteristics, then, does audio have that impact listeners? The distinguishing factor of audio communication outlets from, say, print media outlets is the manipulation of sound. At the most general level, the sequencing of audio news can influence how listeners will perceive the importance and truthfulness of the news, just as is done in television. A contrary news story can be buried further along a news cast, or covered in just a few seconds, while a more favorable news story might be featured first or be given more airtime. The words themselves can be manipulated linguistically as in print: using emotional terms, presenting only one side of an argument, and so on. The power of sound is the intonation and pacing of those words, be they bombastic or hypnotically soothing. Furthermore, digital sounds can be edited down to a single breath to manipulate tonality, timing and loudness as well as taking sound bites out of context and even interspersing different people's speech masked as the original speaker. In effect, these manipulations can lead to audio deepfakes. It can be extremely difficult for the listener to discern these manipulations or trace the audio source. Google's News initiative includes tools to aid fake audio detection.

Manipulation of text and sound constitute content-centric deception and fake news. Other unethical practices that may relate to fake news follow (Berkman, 2008).

- Privacy violations: generalizing from one or two speeches, recording private talk without permission, broadcasting personal information.
- Identity deception: masking one's identity or pretending to be someone else to gain access to a person or great, to steer conversation unethically, or to record audio information.
- Phony authenticity: acting as if one is natural and human, but using it merely as a ruse to win over the audience.
- Manufacturing buzz: consciously trying to hype news or do fake word-of-mouth campaigns to advance fake news.

When people gain good listening skills, practicing audio literacy, they can better discern and understand other people's interests and agendas; a good example is jury duty. In that respect, Dobson (2014) contended that listening, particularly as a democratic process, is best when listeners are open to the speakers and hold their own opinions in abeyance until afterwards when they can reflect and analyze the oral information to determine if it is fake or not.

Audio literacy activities

Here are some resources to hone audio literacy skills in discerning fake visual messages in the news.

- Pearson, J., Nelson, P., Titsworth, S., & Harter, L. (2011). Listening and critical thinking. In *Human communication* (4th ed.). New York, NY: McGraw Hill. https://aclasites.files.wordpress.com/2017/02/judy_pearson_author_paul_nelson_author_scotbookfi-org-copy.pdf
- The anthropology of sound: https://ocw.mit.edu/courses/anthropology/21a-360j-the-anthropology-of-sound-spring-2008/
- Audio Publishers Association literacy activities through audiobooks: www.audiopub.org/teaching-literacy
- Balanced literacy diet: Oral language: www.oise.utoronto.ca/balanced literacydiet/Oral_Language_ELL.html

Data literacy

One of the many methods that fake news creators use to seem credible is the misleading use of data. Many fake news stories include false numerical and textual data, misleading data visualizations, and misleading categorization and other organizational structures. Therefore, it is important to be able to analyze each kind of data accurately and contextually.

Data journalism

Increasingly, data representation and interpretation play an increasingly important role in the news sector, so journalists need to increase their skills in acquiring, evaluating, reproducing and reporting on data. Data journalism has become a significant niche in the field, accounting for 9 percent of all jobs in the news section (Weber & Kosterich, 2018), reflecting specialized training that enables them to provide the data side of news stories and investigate possibly misleading data and data sources. In some cases, data journalism is associated with computer-assisted reporting, particularly in collecting and mining very large data sets. More recently, data visualization using software applications has become part of the field's skill set. In any case, data journalists meld content knowledge, data literacy and communication skills.

Data journalists tend to present data on serious topics such as politics, with entertainment as the secondary emphasis. They largely depend on publicly accessible data such as governmental records rather than gathering raw data themselves. Because data journalists need to employ sophisticated data analysis, they need more in-depth understanding of data structures and analytical methods. In their unique journalistic role, data journalists need to make data understandable to the public, employ transparent processes relative to data, recognize the contexts and objectives of existing data, identify areas of data deficiencies, and uncover data manipulation and data abuse (Loosen, 2018). Thinking like a data journalist can help news consumers recognize misleading and fake data.

Defining data literacy skills

The Oceans of Data Institute (2016) defined a data literate person as one who

> understands, explains, and documents the utility and limitations of data by becoming a critical consumer of data, controlling his/her personal data trail, finding meaning in data, and taking action based on data. The data-literate individual can identify, collect, evaluate, analyze, interpret, present, and protect data.
>
> (p. 2)

The Oceans of Data Institute (2016) further identified the essential skills for data literacy, many of which apply to addressing fake news.

- Formulates product questions.
- Understands the data life cycle.
- Knows about research methods.
- Know about statistical thinking and methods.
- Understands data visualization.
- Is familiar with software such as spreadsheets.
- Thinks analytically, computationally and critically.
- Makes inferences.

Data literacy comprises several sets of skills and ways of thinking, which are defined here.

- Analytical thinking includes clearly defining goals, deconstructing and reconstructing problems to gain insights, and critically exploring patterns in data (Oceans of Data Institute, 2016).
- Numeracy is the ability to understand and use mathematical information.
- Computational thinking involves "formulating problems and their solutions so that the solutions are represented in a form that can be efficiently carried out by an information-processing agent" (Wing, 2011, para. 1).
- Algorithmic thinking involves conceptualizing a solution or task as a series of ordered steps.

Engel (2017) asserted that data science literacy also encompasses elementary statistics, data representation (including visualization) and content knowledge. These aspects certainly help in discerning fake data.

Based on surveying faculty and students about essential data literacy concepts and skills, Carlson and Johnston (2015, pp. 29–30) identified the following core concepts that apply to fake news contexts.

- Is familiar with data formats and data types, especially as they apply to different disciplines.
- Identifies appropriate data sources.
- Understands the data life cycle.
- Recognizes data standards of a field (e.g., metadata, quality, format).
- Utilizes metadata to identify possible problems with data.
- Understands data curation.
- Understands the possible risks and benefits of changing data formats.
- Recognizes incomplete and corrupted data sets.
- Is familiar with basic data analysis tools.
- Is familiar with basic data visualization tools and can identify misleading representations.
- Understands ethical issues related to data use.

By synthesizing several data literary models, Maybee and Zilinski (2015) developed this list of data literacy skills that apply to addressing fake news (p. 2):

- Awareness: understanding data and its role in society.
- Access: identifying, locating and using appropriate data sets and databases.
- Engagement: evaluating, analyzing and interpreting data; making decisions based on data.
- Ethical use: acknowledging data sources, and understanding issues of data reuse.

Statistical literacy

The core concept of data literacy is statistical literacy. Gould (2017) listed several indicators of statistical literacy that apply to fake news discernment.

- Understanding who collects data, as well as why and how they collect it.
- Understanding how data are represented.
- Understanding how data might be altered before its analysis.
- Analyzing and interpreting data.

At any step in the data analytics process fake news creators can fake data, as illustrated in these examples.

- Creating: imagining data, ignoring important variables, using irrelevant variables, asking misleading or loaded questions, cherry-picking subjects.
- Collecting: collecting data from misleading sources, unethically administering a data collection instrument.

- Managing and processing data prior to its use: inappropriately converting data from one format to another, altering or falsifying collected data, cherry-picking supporting data, ignoring or destroying incriminating data or data that does not support the creator's agenda.
- Analyzing and interpreting: making false assumptions or premises, using inappropriate statistical methods, failing to triangulate the data, confusing correlation with causality, making false and misleading interpretations, over-generalizing from a few cases.
- Publishing and dissemination: creating misleading data visualizations, reporting only part of the analysis, "burying" incriminating or contradictory findings, timing the report to maximize negative impact on oppositional stances, using bots to make a fake report go viral.

Such steps can lead to audiences accessing, believing, and making faulty decisions with sometimes disastrous consequences.

Statistical language can also be misleading, as noted below (Mehta & Guzmán, 2018). For instance, the term "thousands" sounds large, but can range from 1001 to 999,999. Assertions about fake data can also include vague terms about probabilities: some, many, multiple, possible, may, likely.

Increasingly, data journalists depend on data mining techniques of large data sets (Shu et al., 2017). Basically, data mining uses digital statistical programs and artificial intelligence to extract information and uncover statistical patterns from very large data sets. While a person could manually process these data, it would be a massive job. Because data mining involves processing data that may be incomplete and unstructured, the data miner might skew the resultant data to confirm desired results. Likewise, as with other statistics, the statistical method used, the analysis and the interpretation of the patterns might be misleading. Sometimes these data sets include private information, and are "mined" without the person's consent. Even though statisticians and data journalists try to anonymous the data, if the data is aggregated in combination, the result may identify an individual possessing a unique set of characteristics (e.g., blind Latina with two adopted children living in 90210). More fundamentally, large data sets are more likely to find significant results, making it easier for fake news creators to cite such findings as a confirmation of their assertions.

STEM data literacy

Data literacy is also part of the larger set of STEM (science, technology, engineering, mathematics) literacies. Pseudo-science is a significant part of fake news, so STEM data literacy is needed to comprehend its content. Peters et al. (2018) categorized science misinformation as originating from scientists (such as those paid by interest groups), commercial sectors (such as drugs that are not well tested), and the general public (such as scares over water fluoridation). In addition, journalists with little scientific background sometimes misrepresent scientific research or do not compare research studies on the same topic.

For instance, health information has become a significant "victim" of fake news as consumers believe online influencers and popular quacks rather than medical professionals (Caulfield et al., 2019). Social media has comprised the major dissemination channel, spreading anti-vaccine rhetoric, virus panicking, and questionable disease treatment strategies. As an example, Mike Adams and his staff of over 15 writers publish up to 15 articles a day for his NaturalNews.com and his other 60 plus websites. These stories range from lemons as effective alternatives to chemotherapy to CO_2 as a positive effect on the environment (McCarthy, 2018). Especially if the fake health news tells a compelling story accompanied by hyped pseudo-data, consumers are likely to follow the bad advice and possibly suffer the consequences. Crowdsourcing of health information, often by non-expert patients, can also sway public opinion, to the detriment of the medical profession – and people's health. As one solution to pseudo-science, scientists are urged to write news articles in language that is comprehensible by the general public, or collaborate with journalists on communicating about science news, to spread their accurate news broadly.

Data visualization

Data journalists increasingly incorporate data visualizations to represent data. Heer, Bostock and Ogievetsky (2010) provided a survey of informative visualization techniques (https://queue.acm.org/detail.cfm?id=1805128). Deciding what way to visualize data depends on the communication objective, as seen in these two websites: https://datavizcatalogue.com/search.html and https://raw.githubusercontent.com/ft-interactive/chart-doctor/master/visual-vocabulary/poster.png.

Data visuals can be easy to manipulate, misleading the consumer to make false conclusions. Yau (2007) visualized one dataset in 25 ways to show how data can be misinterpreted (https://flowingdata.com/2017/01/24/one-dataset-visualized-25-ways/). Wilkinson (2012) identified seven "layers" of data graphics, each of which can be manipulated to mislead the viewer, as noted in accompanying examples (Mehta & Guzmán, 2018).

- Data: the variables to be plotted. Comparing variables that are not mutually exclusive (e.g., West, Central, East, South, Mid-Atlantic); manipulating the timeframe, such as stopping the data before a change in the trend line; showing too few data points, such as missing data points that would change the shape of the graph; burying data by showing too much data such as a line graph of 100 countries (e.g., www.flickr.com/photos/luc/5418037955)
- Esthetics: scale of the data to be mapped. Using misleading colors, such as lighter colors to depict greater density instead of darker colors, expanding, compressing or creating breaks in the y-axis in order to exaggerate – or minimalize – differences, depending on the message's intent.
- Geometrics: shapes that represent the data. In bar graphs, using images such as bodies or trees instead of bars, which exaggerates the quantity (Figure 5.2).

FIGURE 5.2 Visually misleading bar chart

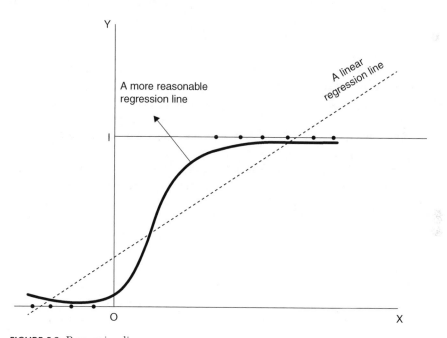

FIGURE 5.3 Regression lines

Based on a graph by Shailaja, K. (CC BY-SA 3.0)

- Statistics: models and summaries. Using a pie chart, which must total 100 percent, but displaying numbers that total more than 100 percent; projecting a false
trajectory of data points (regression analysis states that over time data tends to
regress to the mean, for example, grade point averages are unlikely to continu-
ously improve); assuming a linear regression where a more complex correlation
exists (Figure 5.3)

https://upload.wikimedia.org/wikipedia/commons/8/86/LPM_graph.jpg

- Coordinates: plotting space for the data. Omitting graph labels; omitting the base line (usually of the y-axis).
- Theme: non-data description. Misinterpreting the data and their statistics.

Data literacy education resources and activities

Mandinach and Gummer (2016) used a framework of data use for teaching to identify appropriate skills. Their model works well for identifying skills needed by both teachers and students in inquiring about fake news data (pp. 370–372).

- Identify problems and frame questions. Articulate the issue, and understand its context. Involve stakeholders.
- Use data. Identify possible sources of data, access and retrieve, understand the purposes of different data sources, identify data properties (e.g., scores, composite data, strands, item-level), examine the specificity of data to the issue, determine what data are applicable, determine data quality, determine data accuracy and completeness, examine and drill down into data, analyze data, understand statistics.
- Transform data into information. Consider data's impact and consequences, test assumptions, know how to interpret data, understand data displays and representations, assess patterns and trends, parse probability from causality, articulate inferences and conclusions, summarize and explain data.
- Transform information into decisions. Determine next steps, and understand the context for decisions.
- Evaluate outcomes. Re-examine the original issue, and monitor impact of decisions.

Ridsdale et al. (2015) from Dalhousie University synthesized strategies for data literacy education. Focusing on post-secondary students, the research team recommended teaching about the nature of data, its collection and management, its evaluation, and its application. Not only the concepts but also the mechanics of data literacy should be taught and practiced using real-world data. The teaching strategies should motivate and engage students, connecting learning with personal interests and civic action. The team also stated the need to include all stakeholders and to collaborate between educators and institutions.

Good books that teach data literacy follow.

- Collins, R. (2013). *Weird ways of news.* http://weirdwaysofnews.com/
- *The data journalism handbook 1.* (2012). Maastricht, Netherlands: European Journalism Centre.https://open.umn.edu/opentextbooks/textbooks/the-data-journalism-handbook

- *The data journalism handbook 2.* (2019). Maastricht, Netherlands: European Journalism Centre. www.cimusee.org/mil-resources/learning-resources/the-data-journalism-handbook-2-towards-a-critical-data-practice-2019/
- Fontichiaro, K., Oehrli, J., & Lennex, A. (Eds.). (2019). *Creating data literate students.* Ann Arbor, MI: University of Michigan. http://datalit.sites.uofmhosting.net/books/book/#toc
- Herzog, D. (2016). *Data literacy: A user's guide.* Los Angeles: SAGE.
- Huff, D. (1954). *How to lie with statistics.* New York, NY: Penguin. https://archive.org/details/HowToLieWithStatistics/page/n3/mode/2up
- Steinberg, L. (2017). *Lies, damned lies and statistics: A data literacy primer.* Brussels, Belgium. EAVI. https://eavi.eu/lies-damned-lies-statistics-data-literacy-primer/
- Stray, J. (2016). *The curious journalist's guide to data.* New York, NY: Columbia University. www.cjr.org/tow_center_reports/the_curious_journalists_guide_to_data.php
- Wright, S., Carlson, J. Jeffryes, J., Andres, C. Bracke, M., Fosmire, M., … Westra, B. (2015). Developing data information library programs: A guide for academic librarians. In *Data information literacy.* West Lafayette, IN: Purdue University. www.datainfolit.org/dilguide

Media literacy

News literacy is a subset of media literacy, and media literacy is a subset of information literacy. Media literacy is needed where the information is developed by the mass media, including social media. Mass media's main objective is typically profit, influence or power. In terms of format, mass media can include periodicals as well as broadcasts, film and video. Media often incorporate image, sound and action.

Media literacy may be conceptualized in two ways: in terms of mass media channels, and in terms of media as formats, regardless of the source. When focusing on fake news, the former, more specific, concept serves as an appropriate framework.

Mass media plays a unique communication role. Instead of starting with content that looks for a way to communicate and reach an audience, mass media outlets start with a communication channel, and then look for content to convey. The communication channel then supports a set of media messages. In some cases, the communication channel is created to disseminate specific kinds of information, such as a religious television station. People around the world encounter mass media daily. More than ever, mass media can reach international audiences broadly and deeply. Furthermore, mass media's use of increasingly diverse formats also expands the range of consumers and their levels of understanding. These channels convey messages that reflect and impact social, economic, governmental and religious agendas and processes. Especially as mass media creators are using increasingly sophisticated ways to persuade their audiences, those audiences need to be aware and discerning media consumers (Jolls, 2008).

Each medium represents information using a unique set of features: a unique "language" with its "grammar." People who create fake news in order to get the audience's attention and persuade them to take advantage of such format features, much like advertisers. Especially because mass media has an agenda, individuals need to be aware of their purposes and decide how to respond. In that respect, media literacy for the purposes of this set of literacies focuses on the analysis of the format itself and how it impacts the contained content. The following chart (Table 5.1) compares each medium's critical features, focusing on news. (Less frequent elements are shown in parentheses.)

Television as media

Textual and visual literacy have already been described. Television (TV) is probably the best medium to describe the mix of text, sound and images. O'Donnell's 2016 book on television criticism provides a solid foundation for examining this format.

Television broadcasting consists of regional television stations and national broadcasting networks. In both cases, these outlets either create or access existing television programs. Each show is created by a team of producers, set designers, writers, actors, directors, editors and technical crews. At each point, decision makers can mislead the audience: in selecting the subject matter to broadcast, in choosing the site and designing the set, in scripting fake information, in soliciting or expressing misleading behavior, in editing and sequencing according to an agenda, and filming with bias through lighting, camera angles and cropping. While this team can serve as a check-and-balance for bias or accuracy, top producers have the final say and may reprimand those who do not follow directions.

News shows are typically 30 or 60 minutes long and mix live and pre-recorded segments. Shows usually follow a predictable sequence: breaking news, feature stories, business updates, lifestyle and human-interest stories, sports, weather, commentary, and wrap-up. News may be local, national or international, depending on the station's mission. Television station producers also tend to determine the sequence and balance of the different types of news, which impacts how the audience receives and interprets the information. News talk shows tend to be an hour long, with three to four in-depth stories; increasingly, these shows include panelists or debates to provide different points of view. Most news shows include anchors who announce news and field correspondents.

The average amount of weekday television news programs has increased in the last few years, although the budget for news coverage, especially to pay for staff, has remained stagnant or has declined during the same time period (Anderson, Downie & Schudson, 2016). The audience for watching television news has remained stable, and Americans still prefer to watch the news, mainly through TV, rather than read about it (Mitchell, 2018). Other countries show similar patterns; for instance, most Western Europeans prefer TV news (Matsa, 2018), and Russians get 90 percent of their news through government television (Khaldarova & Pantti, 2016). During that same time period, budgets for TV news in the United States have increased

TABLE 5.1 Medium features, processes and uses

Medium	Format	Features	Process	Use
Books	Print, (audio, tape, digital)	Chapters, text, images (digital can include video, audio)	Write/design > edit > publish	In-depth coverage of a subject, stories
Periodicals (newspapers, magazines, journals)	Print, (Internet)	Headlines, text, images (digital can include videos, audio)	Write/design > edit > publish	Current news, events, entertainment such as comics and games
Radio	Audio	Words, music, other sounds	Write/select > edit > technical broadcast	Current news, interviews, audio arts, talk shows
Podcast	Audio, Internet	Words, music, other sounds	Write/interview/select > edit > technical broadcast	Short personal and group information, news, interviews, audio arts, talk shows
Television	Electronic, (Internet)	Text, sound, still and moving images, use of camera angles and color	Write/visualize > set design > perform > direct > edit > host > technical broadcast	Current news, interviews, documentaries, performances, stories
Movies	Film, video	Sound, sequential moving images, (text), use of camera angles and color	Write/visualize > set design > perform > direct > edit > host > technical production	Documentaries, performances, stories
Video	Electronic: digital, (analog)	Sound, sequential moving images, (text), use of camera angles and color	Script > set design > perform > direct > edit > host > technical production	Current news, interviews, documentaries, performances, stories
Internet	Electronic	Media files: text, sound, images, hyperlinks	Write/select > input > technical broadcast	All of the above
Social media	Internet	Text, sound, images, hyperlinks	Write/select > input > technical broadcast	Short personal and group information

over almost 40 percent of all stations; however, small commercial stations have seen their budgets decrease almost 10 percent. Television news stations tend to rely on advertisements for revenue, with political ads contributing to the stations' economic health in election years. Television stations have also profited from cable and satellite system retransmission fees. These income sources can also impact what news to cover, and what perspective to take; news that conflicts with advertiser sources may result in pulled ads (Mitchell, 2018).

As a multimedia format, television uses many techniques to tell – and "spin" – a news story (O'Donnell, 2016). Television producers communicate their stories, including the news, through social codes that represent reality in commonly understood ways. For instance, objects convey socio-economic status, dialect reflects regionalism, clothing conveys personality, sounds convey mood. Together, the tone, body language and attitude of a news anchor can instill trust and empathy. The technical aspect of television also shapes meaning. For instance, the length of a camera shot can convey relative content importance and intensity of action. How the shot is framed can indicate a sense of epicness for a long shot or intense sincerity for a close-up shot. Reaction shots can reinforce or undermine a statement or action. Natural lighting can convey authenticity, a single light source can make a person seem flat or pale, and minimal light can connote deviousness. These techniques can be leverages to make fake news more believable.

Television viewers also bring their experiences and perspectives when analyzing the news. A basic media literacy tenet is that each person interprets media messages in a unique way. If the person decodes and values the message in the same way as the television producers coded the message and valued it, then there is an accord. However, if the message or messenger represents a dominant culture that differs from the viewers', confusion or tension may result with the viewers not identifying with the news; they have to negotiate that meaning and maybe decide to oppose it (O'Donnell, 2016). On the other hand, a TV producer might want to convince minority viewers of fake news, and deliberately use a spokesperson from that demographic population to convey the message as a way to instill trust and credibility.

O'Donnell (2016) offered useful questions for critically analyzing television programs, including news.

- Orientation. What attracts you to the news program? How do you identify with the news and the reporter? How do you react to the news – and why? Would you share the news with others?
- Narrative. What conventions are used in covering the news? What characters and points of view are presented or omitted? How is conflict played out?
- Organization. What is the structure of the news program? What is the sequence of news items? How do advertisements and their placement impact the news? How are credits handled?
- Demographics. What demographic groups are represented, and what status do they hold? What demographic groups, both as the news force and as the

news subjects, appear to have more power or influence? Who seems to be the intended audience? What demographic do the advertisements tend to target?

- Context. What social and cultural values are represented – or ignored? Is context provided? What seems to be the underlying message or agenda? Does the news reflect the viewer's identity or values?
- Coding. What look and tone do the news programs convey? What are the settings, and what do they connote? What meaning do the sounds connote? What messages do the camera shots convey? What meaning does the lighting connote? What techniques are used to make the viewer believe the news story?

Media literacy for advertising

Mass media largely depends on advertising as a revenue stream. Advertising is communication that promotes or sells an idea, product or service, and may be considered as an agenda-specific subset of mass media. While advertising is not news, its techniques are used by those people who create fake news in order to get the audience's attention and persuade them. Interestingly, advertisers suffer some of the same cynicism as is directed to journalists and politicians, but they still get attention and engender enough trust that people will buy and vote according to the advertising message.

Advertisers identify and learn about their target audience in order to facilitate or inhibit effective communication (O'Shaughnessy & O'Shaughnessy, 2004). The key is to consider the audience's self-image, self-esteem and self-confidence. For instance, advertisers identify values and beliefs in order to support those beliefs or at least not undermine them. They can confirm existing group norms, or they can change people's beliefs if there is a more favorable group that the person wants to join, just as those with higher status: the "winners." How those messages are framed and contextualized facilitates the effectiveness of advertising – and can be used equally well in faking news in order to persuade the audience.

Advertisers use a variety of persuasive techniques, which may be categorized as rational (logo), emotional (pathos) and cultural (ethos) (O'Shaughnessy & O'Shaughnessy, 2004). Any message, such as news, can be made more acceptable by appealing to the audience's beliefs or norms. Focusing on rational strategies, stories can direct attention to certain ideas, definitions can provide the knowledge base, description and classification can change perspectives, analogies can switch thought patterns, visualizations can seem more real, and statistics can provide credibility. Emotional approaches need to be socially acceptable, linking pathos with ethos with terminology that reflects the audience's usage. In addition, advertisers need to enable the audience to emotionally imagine the message or news as symbolic of a benefit that resonates with their current or desired values. The message should also foster a sense of affiliation and solidarity with others, which can boost self-esteem in the process. News consumers can apply these categories as they analyze news.

Audiences also experience a tension between stress-free relaxation and excitement. Therefore, the message, such as news, should provide emotional energy. The optimum state for a rational strategy is calm energy; that state is also conducive for introducing vague or ambiguous language because it can seem intriguing. When the audience is tense, the news should be reassuring and more emotional in nature rather than factual. On the other hand, appeals through fear – such as sickness or isolation – can move a person to change to the advertiser's agenda.

The psychology of behaviorism also operates in advertising, which applies to fake news (O'Shaughnessy & O'Shaughnessy, 2004). For instance, an unconditioned stimulus such as a valued lifestyle linked to the message can make that message valued itself. Other unconscious motives that can be stimulated include affiliation, achievement and power. To reinforce the message, it should be repeated episodically. Adding a new, positive aspect, such as a positive result from the fake news, further conditions the audience. Getting the audience to get involved, such as texting a response or emailing for more information or even volunteering to help, strengthens the impact. To retain audiences, advertisers and fake news creators also need to show the disadvantages of changing sides, including the loss of popularity. If change is the advertiser's and fake news creator's objective, then persuasion should be indirect rather than confrontational in order to ensure that the audience does not lose face. Instead, rhetorical methods such as metaphors and symbolism can de-familiarize the status quo and reorient thinking; they should be accompanied by emotional questions that can raise uncertainty about the current action or belief. Such message creators should also find some common point of agreement, which can be used to pivot thinking. Especially if the audience is not converted, a two-sided appeal leaning to the creator's age will have more impact. Nevertheless, any message should be credible and attractive, even if it is not true. In those cases where the message is questioned or bad-mouthed, that negativism has to be immediately attacked before it can be repeated and eventually believed. News consumers who understand these psychological strategies are less likely to be fooled by fake news.

Media literacy standards

Several organizations have developed media literacy standards, which can relate to fake news. Across the entities, they all address media in society, reading media messages and producing media. In terms of media themselves, common threads include the idea that media creatively mediate reality through each medium's unique structures and "language."

The Center for Media Literacy (www.medialit.org/) identified five constructs that the audience should understand and use when processing media messages (Jolls, 2008):

- Authorship: who created the message.
- Format and techniques of production: techniques used to attract audience attention.
- Audience: how people understand a message differently.

- Content or message: values, lifestyles and points of view represented or omitted.
- Purpose or motive: reason for sending the message.

The National Association for Media Literacy Education (https://namle.net/) identified five media literacy process skills: access, analyze, evaluate, caret, and participate in media. NAMLE suggested six questions to ask:

- Who made the message?
- Why was it made?
- What is missing from the message?
- How might different people interpret it?
- Who might benefit from the message?
- Who might be harmed by the message?

The Canadian Association for Media Literacy (http://aml.ca) developed a framework for teaching media literacy, which included the following key concepts.

- Media construct versions of reality that seem to accurately represent aspects of life.
- Audiences negotiate meanings, which are influenced by their bias and the bias of the messenger.
- Media have economic implications: creation for profit, marketable skills, negative consequences for others.
- Media communicate values, political and social messages.
- Content and format are closely related.
- Each medium has a unique esthetic form.

A leader in media literacy education, Netherland's Mediawijzer.net (Media Pointer) organization identified ten media literacy competencies, grouped into four categories (*10 media literacy competences*, 2011, p. 2).

- Understanding the growing influence of media on society, how media are made, how media color reality.
- Using equipment, software and applications, oriented within media environments.
- Communicating by finding and processing information, creating content, participating in social networks.
- Reflecting on personal media usage, achieving objectives through media.

In 2011 UNESCO developed a media and information literacy curriculum for teachers. The key media literacy outcomes follow (p. 18).

- Understand media's role and function.
- Understand conditions under which media can fulfill their functions.

- Critically evaluate media content in light of media functions.
- Use media for self-expression and civic participation.
- Produce media content.

These standards inform the consumer when discerning fake news.

Funk, Kellner and Share (2016) took a critical approach to media literacy, stating that media literacy involves conceptual understanding of social processes that reflect issues of ideology and power. To that end, they posited six concepts to consider when examining media messages, which can be used to reveal fake news.

- Social constructivism. News is co-constructed and decisions are made along the way within social contexts. People make choices about manipulating content to further their agenda.
- Production and institutions. News creators and organizations shape news to advance their purpose. Fake news not only shapes but manipulates news in an effort to influence audiences.
- Politics of representation. News includes – and omits – values, perspectives and ideologies that support or challenge dominant power. Fake news creators manipulate information to extremes in order to advance their own stance.
- Language and semiotics. Each medium has its unique language and grammar, which impacts how news is constructed, delivered and accessed. Fake news leverages psychological reactions to connotative text and images to influence the audience.
- Audience and positionality. Individuals understand and interpret news within the context of their own experiences and attitudes. Fake news creators analyze the audience's positionality to shape messages that resonate with their audiences.
- Social justice. Media culture perpetuates or challenges ideas about people. Fake news tends to oppose social justice.

Sylvain Timsit (2002) articulated ten strategies for manipulating media, which may serve to guide media analysis.

- Distraction. Distract the public from important issues by flooding them with unimportant information.
- Creating problems then offering solutions. Intensify a situation, such as 9/11, and use it to suggest a solution that advances the manipulator's real agenda.
- Gradual desensitization. Instead of suggesting a sweeping change that would be unacceptable, introduce small innocuous changes bit by bit until the original change is actualized.
- Deferring. Suggest a possible action that is "painful and necessary" but delay it so the public can hope that it doesn't happen – or will be resigned when that action does occur.

- Speaking down. Communicate in a childlike manner so the public will not be as critical or analytical.
- Appealing to the emotional side. Trigger the public's emotions so they will not employ rational thinking.
- Keeping the public ignorant. Don't educate the public about issues – or communication manipulation.
- Encouraging mediocrity and complacency. Encourage anti-intellectualism.
- Reinforcing self-blame. Encourage people to blame themselves for their misfortune rather than place blame on systematic failures.
- Getting to know individuals better than they know themselves. Use biology, sociology and psychology to manipulate the public, but don't share that knowledge with the public.

Media literacy education resources and activities

Here are some useful texts on media literacy education.

- Arnolds-Granlund, S., & Kotilainen, S. (Eds.). (2010). *Media literacy education: Nordic perspectives.* Goteborg, Sweden: Nordicom.
- Baker, F. (2016). *Media literacy in the K-12 classroom* (2nd ed.). Eugene, OR: ISTE.
- Braesel, S., & Karg, T. (2018). *Media and information literacy.* Bonn, Germany: Deutsche Welle.
- DeAbreu, B. et al. (2017). *International handbook of media literacy education.* London: Routledge.
- Fedorov, A. (2015). *Media literacy education.* Moscow, Russia: ICO. www.ifap.ru/library/book564.pdf
- Hobbs, R. (2011). *Digital and media literacy education.* Thousand Oaks, CA: Corwin.
- Marwick, A., & Lewis, R. (2017). *Media manipulation and disinformation online.* New York, NY: Data & Society Research Institute.
- Potter, J. (2016). *Media literacy* (8th ed.). Thousand Oaks, CA: SAGE.
- RobbGrieco, M., & Hobbs, R. (2013). *A field guide to media literacy education in the United States.* Providence, RI: Media Education Lab.
- Silverblatt, A. (2014). *Media literacy* (4th ed.). Santa Barbara, CA: Praeger.
- *Understanding media and culture: An introduction to mass communication.* (2016). Minneapolis, MN: University of Minnesota.
- Wilson, C. et al. (2011). *Media and information literacy curriculum for teachers.* Paris: UNESCO.

Digital literacy

Digital literacy (sometimes called technology literacy or ICT – information and communications technology – literacy) is the ability to use information and communication technologies to safely, responsibly and efficiently find, evaluate, create and communicate information, requiring both cognitive and technical skills. Especially as technology has exponentially expanded formats and dissemination channels, individuals need to be digitally literate to locate, access and critique fake news.

While one could make a case that technology is any human-made tool, generally computers are used as a marker for the first contemporary meaning of technology literacy. Programming was a central computer skill. By the 1990s, computer literacy focused more on using digital software and online applications to access and create knowledge rather than programming and networking. Nowadays, coding has resurfaced as an important competency, though more for developing logical thinking than for developing software or information systems. Belshaw (2011) reviewed the literature on digital literacy, synthesizing his findings into the following digital literacy elements.

- Communicative: understanding how communication media work.
- Confident: understanding problem-solving.
- Cognitive: using cognitive technology tools.
- Constructive: creating with technology.
- Creative: doing new things in new ways.
- Critical: reflecting on digital practices in various semiotic domains.
- Cultural: understanding digital contexts.
- Civic: using technology to support and develop civic society.

Technology in society

One reason that digital literacy has gained credence is the ubiquity of technology in societies globally. Technology's growing spread and sophistication has significantly expanded and quickened the generation of, and access to, information and to people around the world. The consequences range from greater voice and participation in society to increased power and influence by a few conglomerates, from a greater sense of community to increased polarization and feelings of alienation (Balmas, 2014; Ireton & Posetti, 2018). In examining the impact of technology in jobs, Manyika (2017) asserted that 60 percent of all occupations worldwide have at least 30 percent of activities that are technically automatable; many jobs will change and people should expect to use technology as part of their work. Increasingly, governments are using technology to carry out their functions and communicate with their citizens. UNESCO works with countries to show how technology can help educational efforts globally. More generally, the United Nations Commission on Science and Technology, a subsidiary body of the Economic and Social Council, is addressing ways that technological changes can help nations achieve sustainable development goals.

The vast majority of Americans get at least some of their news online, and social media outpaces print newspapers as a news source. Globally, two and a half billion people get news from Facebook (Pew Research Center, 2019b). Especially as seen already, two-thirds of social media users have unwittingly shared fake news, the need for digital literacy is more important than ever.

Digital media production

Technology is also changing the news arena. Most journalists think that digital tools have transformed and improved all aspects of their jobs: from gathering news to production and dissemination processes across different media (Anderson, Downie & Schudson, 2016). Journalists can gather background information and verify facts via the Internet, including online news feeds, or contacting experts online. Most journalists video- or audio-record first-hand news, write up their reports with a word processor, and submit their work online. Data journalists use technology to visualize data to facilitate consumer comprehension (Muratova & Grizzle, 2019). Data analysts using digital algorithms can assess a news story's "clickability," which can impact how a journalist might rewrite a news item to attract more people. Most text and audio/visual editing is done digitally, and even dissemination of the news is now done digitally rather than by analog means. These digital processes can be done more quickly and efficiently than traditional methods (Ireton & Posetti, 2018).

Furthermore, the public is abler to participate in providing information because of low-end technology access. Two-thirds of news organizations distribute content in at least four technology-based formats (Owen, 2019). Thus, the public has more options in accessing the news, not only because of a greater variety of formats, but also because news can often be accessed asynchronously as well as in real time.

While there is talk that entrepreneurs could overtake mainstream news outlets, only about 7 percent of journalists are employed by digital start-ups. Nevertheless, the multiple digital formats and lower access barriers enable more voices to be heard, especially traditionally under-represented populations. Mainstream news outlets are also soliciting news from their constituents via technology such as texting and videos. This kind of participation enriches local news and fosters a more loyal readership.

The picture of digitally-enriched news processes seems like a rosy picture, but those same affordances also enable people to create, produce and disseminate fake news more easily and quickly. The same digital tools that can identify and motivate potential voters can be used to spread false political news (Bruce, 2017). Digital tools such as PhotoShop, Audacity and Adobe Premiere facilitate image and audio manipulation, and sophisticated video tools can create believable deepfake videos. Social media can spread fake news faster than mainstream news outlets, to some extent because of bots and misleading algorithms. Shao et al. (2017) found that accounts that spread fake news tended to be "maintained" by bots. It is relatively easy to create social bots, and much of the 2016 United States Presidential election fake news was generated by bots as well as disseminated by them because they could be shared strategically with likely shared users (Menczer, 2016).

These practices operationalize Couldry's virtues of media practice (2012): accuracy, sincerity and care. As people participate in media production, they need to make sure that the information they communicate is accurate. To that end, they need to find and evaluate existing information, resolve conceptual conflicts, and communicate clearly. Sincerity is the disposition of communicating what one truly believes, and not trying to mislead the target audience; sincerity facilitates trust, which is necessary for exchanging information. Caring about the consequences of communicating information points out the importance of societal accountability – and mutual respect. Especially if one believes in the concept of McLuhan's global village, caring is a necessary condition where survival and growth depend on information interdependence.

Digital literacy standards

Both the name of the literacies associated with the use of technology and their associated competencies vary. In some cases, the emphasis is on learning *about* technology, and in other cases the emphasis is on learning *with* technology. The former focuses on technology as the end goal, and the latter focuses on technology as a means to gain subject matter knowledge. Typically, career education tends to learn about technology as a tool with some attention to its social impact. General education typically examines a learner activity, such as graphing an equation, and seeing what technology can facilitate that function, be it a graphing calculator or a data visualization application.

Synthesizing recognized digital literacy models developed between 2004 and 2014, Iordache, Mariën and Baelden (2017) clustered the competencies into five categories: operational, technical and formal; informational and cognitive; digital communication; digital content creation; and strategic. They found that the models tended to focus on tools-based skills, information literacy skills and communication skills. More recent models mentioned creation, digital identity and data privacy issues to a greater extent than earlier models.

The International Society for Technology in Education (ISTE) developed the most well-known set of digital literacy standards. ISTE's separate but aligned standards exist for students, educators, education leaders and coaches. The 2016 student standards are framed as different digital roles, which can be applied to addressing fake news.

- Empowered learner. Identify and leverage appropriate technology to discern fake news, use technology such as fact-checking tools to seek feedback about evaluating fake news, reflect on the learning process to improve the ability to address fake news.
- Digital citizen. Comply with intellectual property and recognize signs of its abuse, manage one's digital identity and reputation by being mindful about what news to share, manage personal data to maintain digital privacy and security to avoid third-party intrusion that could generate or spread fake news.

- Knowledge constructor. Use effective research strategies to trace fake news sources, evaluate the credibility and perspective of news, curate digital resources to create a collection of reputable news sources, explore real-world issues through reliable news in order to identify feasible solutions.
- Innovative designer. Identify and solve fake news issues by using design thinking and digital tools.
- Computational thinker. Understand how algorithms work to create and disseminate fake news, employ abstract models, use algorithmic thinking and data analysis to discern and deconstruct fake news such as misleading data visualizations.
- Creative communicator. Choose reputable digital platforms and tools to create and communicate news to targeted audiences, create and responsibly remix digital news, communicate complex news by visualizing and modeling it appropriately and responsibly.
- Global collaborator. Use technologies to access and engage with alternative perspectives to counter fake news, use collaborative tools to work with others to address fake news.

The 2017 educator standards also couch literacy in terms of educational roles: as learner, leader, citizen, collaborator, designer, facilitator of learning, and analyst of data.

The International Technology Education Association's 2007 publication *Standards for Technological Literacy: Content for the Study of Technology* clearly focuses on learning about technology, and is most appropriate for STEM (science, technology, engineering, mathematics) applications. Its five standards address the nature of technology, technology's effect on society, design thinking, the designed world (i.e., how technology is used in different work sectors), and abilities such as using and maintaining technology products.

In its support of their sustainable development goals, UNESCO (Law et al., 2018) established a framework of reference for digital literacy skills. They defined digital literacy in terms of knowledge, skills and attitudes, specifically as

> the ability to access, manage, understand, integrate, communicate, evaluate and create information safely and appropriately through digital technologies for employment, decent jobs and entrepreneurship. It includes competences that are variously referred to as computer literacy, ICT literacy, information literacy and media literacy.
>
> (p. 6)

In culling the digital literacy standards of 47 countries, the researchers clustered digital literacy into five competency areas, which apply to fake news.

- Information and data literacy: searching, evaluating and managing data, information and digital content such as fake news.

- Problem-solving of technical problems and incorporating of technologies to solve problems in general, such as using photo editing tools and fact-checking apps to reveal manipulated images.
- Communication and collaboration through digital technologies, such as knowing when to share or "like" news that might be fake.
- Digital content creation, including intellectual property and programming, such as creating accurate news.
- Safety of devices, data, privacy, health and the environment, such as being aware of quack health news scams, news trolling, phishing and intrusive news bots.

It should be recognized that digital literacy has its limits. For instance, even though automated digital techniques can be used to identify some fake news, such technology tools cannot interpret the context of news; it takes human experience and critical thinking skills to verify the credibility of news (Rubin, 2019).

Digital literacy activities

The following websites offer learning opportunities for exploring and practicing digital literacy.

- This bookmark collection lists basic resources on digital literacy: www.merlot. org/merlot/viewPortfolio.htm?id=1245562&hitlist=keywords%3Ddigital%
- This bookmark collection addresses ICT ethical and legal issues: www.merlot. org/merlot/viewPortfolio.htm?id=1038093&hitlist=userId%3D23711%26 2520literacy%26sort.property%3Dlastname%26
- Northeastern University Library digital media toolkit: https://subjectguides. lib.neu.edu/mediakit
- United Kingdom's Jisc digital literacy guide: www.jisc.ac.uk/guides/ developing-digital-literacies
- Here's a fun infographic of educational technology tools created by Kathy Schrock: www.schrockguide.net/uploads/3/9/2/2/392267/edtech_periodic-table.pdf

Information literacy

Information literacy is the core literacy associated with library and information science. Information literacy deals with the location, evaluation, organization, use and communication of information in all formats. Occasionally, information literacy is equated with critical thinking. While critical thinking is certainly involved in these processes, it does not capture some of the skills needed to carry out those processes, such as navigating information systems or using media. Because fake news is communicated in so many ways, the ability to deal with all kinds of information is a central issue and encompasses most of the literacies above.

While the concepts and processes that underlie information literacy have existed for centuries, the term itself dates back to 1974 when Zurkowski used this term in his report for the U.S. National Commission on Library and Information Science. Libraries spearheaded this literacy, which largely consisted of research skills. Since then, the concepts have broadened to the workplace and encompassed greater technology use. By 2003, the United Nations drew together government leaders for a World Summit on the Information Society, at which they made a strong commitment "towards building a people-centred, inclusive and development-oriented Information Society for all, where everyone can access, utilize, and share information and Knowledge" (p. 1). More recently, in 2013, UNESCO has bridged media and information literacies (MIL) as a combined set of competencies with the idea that information is "contained" in media formats, and that a symbiotic relationship exists between the two. The MIL components include access, evaluation and creation.

In the process, UNESCO developed a MIL assessment framework. One of the tiers of UNESCO's framework addresses a country's readiness to support and foster MIL. One of the four indicators for assessing a country's readiness is its media and information supply. UNESCO asserted that "the regulatory mechanisms that prevail in a given country determine the supply of media and the quality of information made available to the population" (p. 52). For instance, are media outlets owned by the state or can they also be owned privately? Who has regulatory authority (e.g., federal or local government, organizations, businesses), and what are their responsibilities? What censorship and filtering regulations and practices exist in the country by government and media outlets? What telecommunications infrastructures exist, who has access to them, and how costly is that access?

Despite international efforts, countries and entities within and across nations continue to have different perspectives about information literacy. As an example, in Germany information literacy has multiple meanings across different domains: communication science, didactics, anthropology, even epistemology (Piloiu, 2016). In general, Germans emphasize the educational role of learning information literacy concepts in order to use and create information; Germans also emphasize the context of knowledge creation and transfer: a culture of knowledge that also speaks to the importance of self-understanding of worldview interpretation.

Information literacy for producing the news

The idea of information literacy at both the individual and public tiers certainly applies to the news sector, including fake news. As a reminder, fake news is deliberately false; its creators purport such news to be true in order to mislead the news audience; thus, fake news creators need to be information literate as well as ethical news creators.

At the tier one level, as defined by UNESCO's MIL framework, the news outlet as a whole needs to provide access to communications channels and a way to retrieve information from those channels for their staff as well as for their audience. They usually need to follow regulations to establish and maintain those channels in a responsible manner, which entails information literacy to identify those regulations and how to access and comply with them. They need information literacy in creating a mechanism to evaluate and select the news to communicate, and may need to comply with regulations as to acceptable content such as a balanced approach to news or news dissemination restrictions relative to high-security classified information. News outlets also need information literacy to organize news content effectively for audience engagement. The news outlet's creation and communication of news is the audience's access; the news outlet needs information literacy in order to communicate effectively, with the knowledge of their potential audience's information literacy level to access and comprehend that communicated news. Furthermore, news outlets need information literacy to monitor their processes and the reactions of their audiences in order to improve their efforts and impact.

At the tier two level, individuals within the news organization each need information literacy in order to carry out their specific news functions. In terms of news access and retrieval, journalists have to define their news information task, identify what information they need and likely sources of that information, and then access and retrieve that information. Retrieval might include attending events, interviews, scouring existing documents and artifacts, using databases, taking photographs and filming situations. Photographers and film crews need information literacy in order to determine what to record and how to capture the moment in compelling ways. Production crews need to use information literacy to know how to access and retrieve those news documents so they can be processed. Even the facilities managers and set designers need information literacy in order to determine what kind of setting is needed, what sources of set materials are available, and how to acquire those materials as well as human resources who can manually or virtually create those sets. The news director has the ultimate responsibility for determining what human and material resources are needed, including finances, and how to acquire them. This responsibility requires deep and broad operations and networking knowledge and skills.

In terms of news understanding and evaluation, journalists need subject knowledge and communication theory understanding. They also need to apply critical thinking to analyze the quality of the news information that they gather. Production editors also need subject knowledge and communication theory in order to determine how to process the news documents: determining the importance of each news item for possible inclusion in the final news product, editing the material to fit the time or space limitations such that the vital information is included, and organizing the selected material for maximum attention and engagement by the identified audience. Facilities managers need information literacy to understand how physical space impacts how news is processed, such as the state of the equipment and the working area for production and collaboration. The news director has the ultimate responsibility for understanding and evaluating the entire operation: of staff, materials, facilities, and the budget for making all those parts possible.

In terms of creating and sharing, journalists need information literacy to determine the most effective way to communicate news, including how each medium shapes the message. They also need to know how to use the tools to communicate those news messages. The production crew needs information literacy as they operate the machinery and other technologies to create and disseminate the final periodical issue, radio or TV show, or social media product. The facilities managers also need information literacy to monitor the physical space and supporting technology to ensure that the communication processes run smoothly. The news director has the ultimate responsibility for monitoring the entire operation's creation and implementation, which requires critical analysis and effective allocation of resources.

Creators and disseminators of fake news need just as much information literacy as reputable news outlets. They need information literacy to determine their information agenda, their target audience, and the information needed to persuade their audience. They need information literacy in order to access and retrieve information, mainly to advance their agenda. In the process of selecting and evaluating that information, they also need to know the opposition's point of view, an important information literacy skill, and how to extract part of that information to then "spin" or reframe that information to support their own perspective. In creating fake news, they need to know how to communicate convincingly, which entails knowledge of information behaviors and rhetoric. In the process, fake news creators need information literacy to determine which medium is most effective for reaching their target audience and convincing them. Furthermore, they need information literacy in order to monitor audience access and reaction so they can finesse their message for optimum influence.

The more that news consumers know how information literacy drives news production, the more informed news consumers can be in knowing how to access and retrieve news sources, evaluate those news sources, and share news and participate in news creation.

Information literacy issues related to fake news

Throughout the process of addressing fake news, individuals encounter several issues. Even without proactively seeking news, people can feel overwhelmed. Not only do they lack the time to pay attention to every news item, but to assess every news item can be mentally and psychologically taxing. In such situations, users tend to respond more to emotional headlines, friends' communications, news that confirms their existing views, or their own interests (Ciampaglia & Menczer, 2018; Cohen & Mihailidis, 2012; Head et al., 2018).

Even when searching for true news, individuals can have difficulty locating reputable news, particularly when the topic is controversial and awash with fake news. Finding the kernels of truth can be daunting. In those cases, information literate individuals can usually rely on those media outlets that they have found over time to consistently disseminate reputable news that contains substantiated evidence (Zubiaga et al., 2015).

Even the stability of a news item has come under scrutiny as dynamic sources have become more common. News validity can be questioned as websites and social media can change at any time, especially when multiple individuals can edit those sites. Even videos can be edited and updated with relative ease. Which version is correct? Increasingly, mainstream journalists are under pressure to blast out news quickly in order to beat the competition. In the process, journalists lack enough time and resources to verify facts let alone get all the information to provide a complete picture. Furthermore, as events unfold, situations change and new facts emerge or existing information is found to be incorrect. For those reasons, news stories are updated as conditions change. However, minor stories might not get such updated treatment, sometimes leaving the audience with a wrong first impression. At the same time, audiences cannot be expected to check daily to see if a news story has changed. This conundrum is hard to resolve. Probably, the best solution is for individuals to wait out the news to see what finally "settles" as the whole story. Usually it is the significant news story that will eventually get richer commentary and in-depth analysis. Those same stories also "shake out" fake news, like a harvest sifting the wheat from the chaff. Information literate people try to practice patience rather than jump on immediate viral, often fake, news. On the other hand, squelching fake news before it spreads is also a good practice; the safest route is not to share doubtful news in any case. This is another instance when waiting for the news to come to a person is more beneficial than seeking out early news.

Information literacy models and standards for the news consumer

Several library organizations have developed information literacy models and standards, which can be applied when addressing fake news. Information literacy models show the structure and elements of information literacy, and standards state the level of competencies needed to achieve information literacy. Some models and standards are targeted to specific audiences and others are more general. Other organizations use another term besides standards, such as guidelines. Traditionally, information literacy standards have focused on research processes and skills. For instance, the 2000 Association of College and Research Libraries (ACRL) information literacy standards, which traced research processes, served as the basis for several countries' information literacy standards (ACRL, 2017). More recently, some organizations, as seen in UNESCO's MIL framework, blend information literacy with other literacies or couch information literacy in terms of general learning skills, as approached by the American Association of School Librarians (AASL). These variations highlight the ambiguity of information literacy.

For instance, in 2015 ACRL switched from standards to a framework of six information literacy frames, which may be employed to discern fake news.

- Authority is constructed and contextual. Who created the news item? What is the reason for the news item; why is it being created? What is the context for its creation?

- Information creation as a process. How was the news item developed? How transparent is that process? What are the sources of information, and are they cited? Who monitors and edits the news item? How is that news item selected and presented for dissemination? What news channel is used to disseminate the information? What is the timeframe for creating and disseminating the news item?
- Information has value. What benefit do the creator and disseminator derive from this news item: money, publicity, prestige, power, influence, change? What benefit does the audience derive from the news item: information, insider privilege and status?
- Searching as strategic exploration. What questions should you ask about the news item? What are the possible sources of information? What key words will define the search? How might one source lead to another source for additional insight into the news item?
- Research as inquiry. What is the background of the news item? What or who is the source of the news? What information is included, and what information is omitted?
- Scholarship as conversation. What might be other perspectives about the news item? How do other media outlets treat that same news topic? Who is sharing the information; what is their credibility and agenda?

SCONUL (Society of College, National and University Libraries) identified seven pillars of information literacy that define abilities and understandings of information literacy development in higher education (Bent & Stubbings, 2011). The model is not linear but rather describes the information world and a person's engagement with that world; however, the framework still reflects an academic research approach. Those pillars, which follow, may be used in discerning and addressing fake news.

- Identify a personal need for information, such as keeping current with news in general, seeking news about a specific topic such as politics or emergencies, or determining if a news item is fake or not.
- Scope out current knowledge and identify gaps in order to determine the type of news available and those characteristics of different news sources.
- Plan strategies for locating news by comparing search tools, using controlled vocabularies, and revising strategies.
- Gather the needed news by understanding how information is organized, realizing the issues involved in collecting news (e.g., the difference between free and paid-for news sources).
- Evaluate the research process, and compare the news resources in terms of their quality, process of development, and context.
- Manage news responsibly in terms of organizing, storing and sharing it.
- Present the results of news investigation by synthesizing findings, creating knowledge, and disseminating it.

Dorner and Gorman (2006) asserted that most information literacy models and standards are based on Western cultural values and assumptions, and questioned those models' viability in developing countries, which have different social contexts. They argued that Western information literacy actually builds on a deficiency model: that one lacks and needs external information so must learn the appropriate skills to seek and comprehend that information. Dorner and Gorman posited that information literacy should recognize the "social construction and cultural authority of knowledge" as well as the "political economy of knowledge ownership and control" (p. 5), which then impacts the access and understanding of that information. That recognition thus shapes individuals' critique of information, integrating it into their current knowledge base, and using it to address their own needs. Dorner and Gorman further stated that information literacy needs to acknowledge the context of people's unique ways of feeling, learning and communicating. When information literacy is taught in formal education, when those institutional values conflict with personal values, learners have to negotiate those differences and may compartmentalize those values such that they act situationally rather than on underlying principles. In that respect, such individuals are more likely to contextualize fake news in terms of where they encounter it and who is communicating that news; those contexts are apt to influence how individuals will perceive and act upon the fake news. The more aware that news consumers are of those contexts, including their own situations, the more informed they are, in effect.

Other information literacy models and standards focus more on social issues, which reflects much of fake news agendas. Critical information literacy exemplifies this approach, and often delves into power relationships involved in information, such as news, production and dissemination. The intent is to empower individuals to become active agents of change in their society. This attitude about information literacy is particularly relevant to developing nations and post-conflict regions. In his review of critical information literacy models, Tewell (2015) determined that critical information literacy models examine "the social construction and political dimensions of information, and problematizes information's development, use, and purposes with the intent of prompting students to think critically about such forces and act upon this knowledge" (p. 36). Critical information literacy is very relevant for discerning fake news as it asks about the reasons for creating news, the processes for its development, and its social-political consequences. While news consumers should be open-minded about the news they encounter, they should also keep a skeptical mindset. Critical information literacy also calls upon consumers to proactively act upon news, which might entail exposing fake news and providing true news to counteract fake news as well as acting upon real news.

Information literacy activities

The following websites offer learning opportunities for exploring and practicing information literacy, largely for evaluating sources.

- The complete guide to evaluating online resources. (2019). *HostingFacts.* https://hostingfacts.com/evaluating-online-resources/
- *Fake news, misleading news, biased news: Evaluating sources.* (2019). Hillsborough, FL: Hillsborough Community College. https://libguides.hccfl.edu/fakenews/evaluatingsources
- Hisle, D., & Webb, K. (2017). *Information literacy concepts: An open educational resource.* Greenville, NC: East Carolina University.
- *Information literacy & fake news.* (2020). Frankfort, KY: Kentucky Virtual Library. https://kyvl.org/c.php?g=624628&p=4358010
- Information Literacy Group. (2020). *Fake news – Information literacy.* London, UK: Information Literacy Group.
- *Information literacy in an era of alternative facts & fake news.* (2019). Philadelphia, PA: Temple University. https://guides.temple.edu/c.php?g=646455&p=4534956

References

10 media literacy competences. (2011). Amsterdam, Netherlands: Mediawijzer.

Anderson, C., Downie, L., & Schudson, M. (2016). *The news media: What everyone needs to know.* New York, NY: Oxford University Press.

Association of College and Research Libraries. (2000). *Information literacy competency standards for higher education.* Chicago, IL: Association of College and Research Libraries.

Association of College and Research Libraries. Working Group on Global Perspectives for Information Literacy, Student Learning and Information Literacy Committee. (2017). *Global perspectives on information literacy: Fostering a dialogue for international understanding.* Chicago, IL: Association of College and Research Libraries.

Balmas, M. (2014). When fake news becomes real: Combined exposure to multiple news sources and political attitudes of inefficacy, alienation, and cynicism. *Communication Research, 41*(3), 430–454.

Belshaw, D. (2011). What is digital literacy? A pragmatic investigation. Doctoral dissertation. Durham University.

Bent, M., & Stubbings, R. (2011). *The SCONUL seven pillars of information literacy.* London, UK: SCONUL.

Berkman, R. (2008). *The art of strategic listening: Finding market intelligence through blogs and other social media.* Ithaca, NY: Paramount Market Publishing.

Berry, R. (2016). Podcasting: Considering the evolution of the medium and its association with the word "radio". *The Radio Journal International Studies in Broadcast and Audio Media, 14*(1), 7–22.

Braesel, S., & Karg, T. (2018). *Media and information literacy.* Bonn, Germany: Deutsche Welle. www.dw.com/downloads/42424317/dw-akademiemilguidebook2018.pdf

Bruce, P. (2017, March 2). When the big lie meets big data. *Scientific American.* https://blogs.scientificamerican.com/guest-blog/when-the-big-lie-meets-big-data/

Carlson, J., & Johnston, L. (2015). *Data information literacy: Librarians, data, and the education of a new generation of researchers.* West Lafayette, IN: Purdue University Press.

Carlson, M. (2009). The reality of a fake image: News norms, photojournalistic craft, and Brian Walski's fabricated photograph. *Journalism Practice, 3*(2), 125–139.

Caulfield, T., Marcon, A. R., Murdoch, B., Brown, J. M., Perrault, S. T., Jarry, J., … & Rachul, C. (2019). Health misinformation and the power of narrative messaging in the public sphere. *Canadian Journal of Bioethics/Revue canadienne de bioéthique, 2*(2), 52–60.

Ciampaglia, G., & Menczer, F. (2018, June 21). Biases make people vulnerable to misinformation spread by social media. *Scientific American.* www.scientificamerican.com/article/biases-make-people-vulnerable-to-misinformation-spread-by-social-media/

Cohen, J., & Mihailidis, P. (2012). Storify and news curation: Teaching and learning about digital storytelling. In *Second annual social media technology conference & workshop* (Vol. 1, pp. 27–31). Washington, DC: Howard University.

Couldry, N. (2012). *Media, society, world: Social theory and digital media practice.* Cambridge, UK: Polity.

Dobson, A. (2014). *Listening for democracy.* Oxford, UK: Oxford University Press.

Dorner, D. G., & Gorman, G. E. (2006). Information literacy education in Asian developing countries: Cultural factors affecting curriculum development and programme delivery. *IFLA Journal, 32*(4), 281–293.

Dubber, A. (2013). *Radio in the digital age.* Cambridge, UK: Polity Press.

Engel, J. (2017). Statistical literacy for active citizenship: A call for data science education. *Statistics Education Research Journal, 16*(1), 44–49.

Funk, M. (2017). Decoding the podaissance: Identifying community journalism practices in newsroom and avocational podcasts. *International Symposium on Online Journalism, 7*(1), 67–87.

Funk, S., Kellner, D., & Share, J. (2016). Critical media literacy as transformative pedagogy. In M. Yildiz & J. Keengwe (Eds.), *Handbook of research on media literacy in the digital age* (pp. 1–30). Hershey, PA: IGI Global.

Geise, L., & Baden, C. (2014). Putting the image back into the frame: Modeling the linkage between visual communication and frame-processing theory. *Communication Theory, 25*(1), 46–69.

Gervais, T. (2010). Witness to war: The uses of photography in the illustrated press: 1855–1904. *Journal of Visual Culture, 9*(3), 370–384.

Gould, R. (2017). Data literacy is statistical literacy. *Statistics Education Research Journal, 16*(1), 22–25.

Hall, H. K. (2018). Deepfake videos: When seeing isn't believing. *Catholic University Journal of Law & Technology, 27,* 51–76.

Head, A., Wihbey, J., Metaxas, P., MacMillan, M., & Cohen, D. (2018). *How students engage with news: Five takeaways for educators, journalists, and librarians.* Chicago, IL: Association of College and Research Libraries.

Hedgecoe, J. (2009). *New manual of photography.* London, UK: Dorling Kindersley Ltd.

Heer, J., Bostock, M., & Ogievetsky, V. (2010). A tour through the visualization zoo. *Graphics, 8*(5). https://queue.acm.org/detail.cfm?id=1805128

International Society for Technology in Education. (2016). *ISTE standards for students.* Eugene, OR: International Society for Technology in Education.

International Society for Technology in Education. (2017). *ISTE standards for educators.* Eugene, OR: International Society for Technology in Education.

International Technology Education Association. (2007). *Technological literacy standards: Content for the study of technology* (3rd ed.). Reston, VA: International Technology Education Association.

Iordache, C., Mariën, I., & Baelden, D. (2017). Developing digital skills and competences: A quick-scan analysis of 13 digital literacy models. *Italian Journal of Sociology of Education, 9*(1), 6–30.

Ireton, C., & Posetti, J. (2018). *Journalism, "fake news" & disinformation.* Paris: UNESCO.

Jolls, T. (2008). *Literacy for the 21st century: An overview & orientation guide to media literacy education* (2nd ed.). Santa Monica, CA: Center for Media Literacy.

Khaldarova, I., & Pantti, M. (2016). Fake news: The narrative battle over the Ukrainian conflict. *Journalism Practice*, *10*(7), 891–901.

Kovach, B., & Rosenstiel, T. (2010). *Blur: How to know what's true in the age of information overload*. New York, NY: Bloomsburg.

Lacey, K. (2013). Listening in the digital age. In J. Loviglio & M. Hilmes (Eds.), *Radio's new wave: Global sound in the digital age* (pp. 9–23). New York, NY: Routledge.

Law, N., Woo, D., de la Torre, J., & Wong, G. (2018). *A global framework of reference on digital literacy skills for indicator 4.4.2*. Montreal, Quebec: UNESCO Institute for Statistics. http://uis.unesco.org/sites/default/files/documents/ip51-global-framework-reference-digital-literacy-skills-2018-en.pdf

Loosen, W. (2018). Data-driven gold-standards: What the field values as award-worthy data journalism and how journalism co-evolves with the datafication of society. In J. Gray, L. Chambers, & L. Bounegru (Eds.), *The data journalism handbook* (p. 2). Maastricht, Netherlands: European Journalism Centre. https://datajournalism.com/read/handbook/two/situating-data-journalism/data-driven-gold-standards-what-the-field-values-as-award-worthy-data-journalism-and-how-journalism-co-evolves-with-the-datafication-of-society

Maksl, A., Ashley, S., & Craft, S. (2015). Measuring news media literacy. *Journal of Media Literacy Education*, *6*(3), 29–45.

Mandinach, E., & Gummer, E. (2016). What does it mean for teachers to be data literate: Laying out the skills, knowledge, and dispositions. *Teaching and Teacher Education*, *60*, 366–386.

Manyika, J. (2017) *Technology, jobs, and the future of work*. New York, NY: McKinsey Global Institute.

Matsa, K. (2018, September 27). Most Western Europeans prefer TV news while use of print outlets lags. *FactTank*. www.pewresearch.org/fact-tank/2018/09/27/most-western-europeans-prefer-tv-news-while-use-of-print-outlets-lags/

Maybee, C., & Zilinski, L. (2015). *Data informed learning: A next phase data literacy framework for higher education*. Presentation for ASIST Conference, November 6–15, St. Louis, MO.

McCarthy, J. (2018, May 3). Far from natural. *The Weather Channel*. https://features.weather.com/far-from-natural/

Mehta, R., & Guzmán, L. D. (2018). Fake or visual trickery? Understanding the quantitative visual rhetoric in the news. *Journal of Media Literacy Education*, *10*(2), 104–122.

Menczer, F. (2016, November 28). Fake online news spreads through social echo chambers. *Scientific American*. www.scientificamerican.com/article/fake-online-news-spreads-through-social-echo-chambers/

Mitchell, A. (2018). *Americans still prefer watching to reading the news – and most still through television*. Washington, DC: Pew Research Center.

Morra, J., & Smith, M. (Eds.). (2006). *Visual culture*. New York, NY: Routledge.

Muratova, N., & Grizzle, A. (2019). *Media and information literacy in journalism: A handbook for journalists and journalism educators*. Tashkent, Uzbekistan: Baktria Press.

Newman, N., & Gallo, N. (2019, December 3). News podcasts and the opportunities for publishers. *Digital News Report*. www.digitalnewsreport.org/publications/2019/news-podcasts-opportunities-publishers/

Oceans of Data Institute. (2016). *Building global interest in data literacy: A dialogue*. Waltham, MA: Educational Development Center.

O'Donnell, V. (2016). *Television criticism* (3rd ed.). Thousand Oaks, CA: SAGE.

O'Shaughnessy, J., & O'Shaughnessy, N. (2004). *Persuasion in advertising*. New York, NY: Routledge.

Otero, V. (2017). The chart, version 3.0: What, exactly, are we reading? *Ad Fontes Media*. www.adfontesmedia.com/the-chart-version-3-0-what-exactly-are-we-reading/ ?v=402f03a963ba

Owen, D. (2019). *The state of technology in global newsrooms*. Washington, DC: International Center for Journalists.

Pearson, J., Nelson, P., Titsworth, S., & Harter, L. (2011). Listening and critical thinking. In *Human communication* (4th ed.). New York, NY: McGraw Hill. https://aclasites.files. wordpress.com/2017/02/judy_pearson_author_paul_nelson_author_scotbookfi-org-copy.pdf

Peters, A., Tartari, E., Lotfinejad, N., Parneix, P., & Pittet, D. (2018). Fighting the good fight: The fallout of fake news in infection prevention and why context matters. *Journal of Hospital Infection, 100*(4), 365–370.

Pew Research Center. (2019a). *Audio and podcasting fact sheet.* Washington, DC: Pew Research Center.

Pew Research Center. (2019b). *Digital news fact sheet.* Washington, DC: Pew Research Center.

Piloiu, R. (2016). Rethinking the concept of "information literacy": A German perspective. *Journal of Information Literacy, 10*(2), 78–93.

Potter, W. (2010). The state of media literacy. *Journal of Broadcasting & Electronic Media, 54*(4), 675–696.

Ridsdale, C., Rothwell, J., Smit, M., Ali-Hassan, H., Bliemel, M., Irvine, D., … & Wuetherick, B. (2015). *Strategies and best practices for data literacy education: Knowledge synthesis report.* Halifax, NS: Dalhousie University.

Rubin, V. L. (2019). Disinformation and misinformation triangle: A conceptual model for "fake news" epidemic, causal factors and interventions. *Journal of Documentation, 75*(5), 1013–1034.

Schwartz, A. (2015). *Broadcast hysteria: Orson Welles's War of the Worlds and the art of fake news.* New York, NY: Macmillan.

Shao, C., Ciampaglia, G. L., Varol, O., Flammini, A., & Menczer, F. (2017, July 24). The spread of fake news by social bots. *arXiv* preprint 1707.07592, 96–104.

Shu, K., Sliva, A., Wang, S., Tang, J., & Liu, H. (2017). Fake news detection on social media: A data mining perspective. *ACM SIGKDD Explorations Newsletter, 19*(1), 22–36.

Tewell, E. (2015). A decade of critical information literacy: A review of the literature. *Communications in Information Literacy, 9*(1), 24–43.

Timsit, S. (2002). *Stratégies de manipulation.* www.syti.net/Manipulations.html

UNESCO. (2013). *Media and information literacy assessment framework: Country readiness and competencies.* Paris, France: UNESCO.

United Nations. (2003). *Declaration of principles: Building the information society: A global challenge in the new millennium.* Paris, France: United Nations.

Webb, J. (2020). *Design principles for photography* (2nd ed.). New York, NY: Bloomsbury Visual Arts.

Weber, M., & Kosterich, A. (2018). Number crunching. *Columbia Journalism Review, 57*(2), 106–110.

Wierzbicka, A. (2005). There are no "color universals" but there are universals of visual semantics. *Anthropological Linguistics, 47*(2), 217–244.

Wilkinson, L. (2012). The grammar of graphics. In J. Gentle, W. Härdle, & Y. Mori (Eds.), *Handbook of computational statistics* (pp. 375–414). Berlin, Germany: Springer.

Wing, J. (2011, March). Research notebook: Computational thinking—what and why? *The LINK.* www.cs.cmu.edu/link/research-notebook-computational-thinking-what-and-why

Wolvin, A., & Cohen, S. (2012). An inventory of listening competency dimensions. *International Journal of Listening, 26,* 24–26.

Worth, S., & Adair, J. (1972). *Through Navajo eyes: An exploration in film communication and anthropology.* Bloomington, IN: Indiana University Press.

Yau, N. (2007). One dataset, visualized 25 ways. *FlowingData.* https://flowingdata.com/2017/01/24/one-dataset-visualized-25-ways/

Zubiaga, A., Spina, D., Martínez, R., & Fresno, V. (2015). Real-time classification of twitter trends. *Journal of the Association for Information Science and Technology, 66*(3), 462–473.

Zurkowski, P. (1974). *The information service environment – Relationships and priorities.* Washington, DC: U.S. Commission on Libraries and Information Science.

6

THE CIVIC ENGAGEMENT CONTEXT

Too often fake news is framed as a consumer issue, with a caveat about sharing such disinformation. Fake news is something that should be acknowledged, but more importantly addressed and countered. Fake news can even serve as a catalyst to become more civically engaged. Especially with the advances in social media, fake news points out the need for digital citizenship: supporting and acting upon reputable news.

Civic engagement

Civic engagement may be defined as individual and collective actions that identify and address issues of public concern. The underlying goal is to improve the quality of life within a community through actions that may be political or non-political. Civic engagement can occur at any stage of policy-making and implementation: from agenda-setting and analysis, through planning and implementation, to monitoring. Voting and campaigning, volunteering and service learning, community-improvement projects such as cleaning beaches and maintaining food banks, and actively advocating for human rights are typical examples of civic engagement. The United States Department of Education (2012) listed newer civic engagement forms: innovation and entrepreneurship, dialogue across differences, and global learning.

It should be noted that the terms "citizen" and "citizenship" do not appear in this definition or its operationalization. A citizen may be strictly defined as a person who is a legally recognized subject of a state or nation, who has the rights and protection of that government. More broadly, the concept of a citizen applies to any member of a community. Citizenship, then, refers to rights and responsibilities as a participating member of the community. In analyzing civic websites, Freelon, Wells and Bennett (2013) found that today's youth have a sense of different citizen identity from previous generations. Rather than seeing citizenship as a duty, contemporary youth see it as a self-actualizing activity through social expression in self-defined loosely-coupled networks.

Models of civic engagement

Westheimer and Kahn (2004) posited three models of citizenship and civic engagement, each of which may be linked to fake news.

- **Personally responsive citizens** should obey laws and act responsibly. They should also keep abreast of current events in order to make informed decisions. In terms of fake news, individuals should not create fake news; that act is basically immoral. Individuals should not share fake news either, which means that they need to be able to judge the credibility and accuracy of news before deciding how to act on news. Knowledgeable citizens can instead screen fake news and inhibit its spread. At the same time, they might well share true news stories to inform others. Another action step is responding to fake news. Typically, counter examples are usually more effective than direct contradiction (Haigh, Haigh & Kozak, 2018). Instead of debating an issue in a traditional pro-con "winner" way, individuals can instead try to find the reasons for a particular stance (Pogue, 2017), and find some common truth that might override fake news. Personally responsive citizens might also volunteer in the community, such as bringing food to the elderly or ushering at church.
- **Citizen deliberation and participation** implies interaction with others. Responding to polls and surveys about social issues such as fake news is a low-stakes action. Individuals might write letters or email legislators about some social concern, such as the lack of education about fake news. They might exchange ideas with others about the consequences of fake news. They might also participate in groups and collaborate with them for a common good, such as creating infographics about ways to discern fake news.
- **Social justice-oriented citizens** seek social justice as a moral imperative, be it to ensure human rights or equity and fairness. At this level of engagement, individuals need the knowledge and skills to effect social change that can be sustained. In terms of fake news, such reform might entail working with educators to develop a social justice curriculum that addresses fake news (Pennell & Fede, 2018).

A relatively new movement has broadened the concept of civic engagement: participatory politics. Participatory politics may be defined as interactive, peer-based acts to voice and influence issues of public concern, such as fake news (Cohen et al., 2012). Jenkins (2009) defined several forms of participatory culture: affiliation of online communities, expressions of new creative forms, collaborative problem-solving, and circulation of media flow. Kahne, Hodgin and Eidman-Aadahl (2016) identified core civic engagement practices: investigation and research, dialogue and feedback, production and circulation, and mobilizing for change.

Digital media has gained popularity as a mode of political engagement, thanks to easy access and production; fewer gatekeepers control or constrain participation, which particularly impacts traditionally marginalized populations. People can use new media to act more independently to negotiate with power, reach and mobilize audiences and networks, shape agendas through dialogue with decision-makers, exert greater agency through sharing and generating political information. Participatory culture also leverages social connections (Kligler-Vilenchik & Shresthova, 2012). Individuals learn from their peers and mentors, and build on shared passion to form a sense of community and group identity. People of all ethnicities can partici- pate, and gain digital social capital (e.g., knowledge, skills, networks) in the process. Females, in particular, have more opportunities to develop techno-social literacies that help them use technology for societal impact, such as digital storytelling to address consequences of fake news (Middaugh & Kirshner, 2015).

At the same time that participatory politics encourages broad-based voices, access to civic opportunities faces significant equity issues (Kahne, Hodgin & Eidman- Aadahl, 2016). Schools in lower socio-economic neighborhoods often do not have adequate technology infrastructure or technical support, and what technology is available is often used to teach basic skills. Furthermore, educators need to address the challenges of diversity. What are the cultural and gendered values and norms that shape civic participation? How do hegemonic power and privilege impact interaction and mobilization? Educators need to heed students' self-identities and social contexts, and impress upon the importance of positionality in both teaching and supporting participatory politics.

Middaugh and Kirshner also recognized that participatory politics may limit access for youth outside of formal education who may be ignored or marginalized; misinformation and disinformation may increase, and youth may conflate voice and influence. Therefore, media literacy needs to be taught; people need opportunities and guidance in creating and disseminating informed and persuasive media effect- ively to counteract fake news. People need broad and equitable access to media infrastructures, resources and support to discern fake news. At the systemic level, political social issue groups need to leverage the expertise and insights of youth and other populations to address fake news. Examples of participatory politics that can address fake news include blogs, infographics, creation of global dialogues, app development, digital testimonials and documentary filmmaking, among other initiatives.

Impact of civic engagement

Civic engagement benefits both the community or more specific recipient of that engagement as well as the engaged individual or group. Civically engaged individ- uals gain a greater sense of belonging and purposefulness. They also improve social skills and problem-solving abilities. All of these actions result in greater social capital, that is, the value of interpersonal relationships and their resources as they contribute to society. In the context of fake news, social capital can make or break fake news. Repeated sharing by trusted people, which can be a form of civic engagement, can give fake news social currency. What is needed is social capital and solidarity *against* fake news and *for* authentic news. That kind of civic engagement can improve society rather than polarize it (D'Costa, 2016).

Everyone is a stakeholder in civic engagement because each one is impacted by such action: through legislation, allocated resources (material, human and fiscal), education, services, and daily interaction. While governmental leaders tend to be considered as the main beneficiaries of civic engagement, they allocate resources for their constituents and they serve at the pleasure of those constituents who easily voice their satisfaction by voting and other civic engagement. For voters to make informed decisions, either in the voting booth or other civic action, they need to access and evaluate information critically and civically. Those actions depend on news outlets and educators. Furthermore, all individuals impact their community through their actions or inactions: maintaining the physical conditions of their neighborhoods, sustaining their families, interacting with others, contributing their work and time, and making good use of allocated resources. All of these stakeholders, again, depend on accurate and thorough information; fake news leads to poor decisions – or cynicism and social withdrawal.

On a more granular level, each economic sector and each profession is a stakeholder and potential agent in civic engagement. Formal and informal education is an obvious example. Educators provide opportunities for learners to practice civic education through service-oriented co-curriculum, service learning, and community-based work-study placements. Educators provide civic education and encourage students to explore and pursue public service careers. Educators also promote and facilitate family participation in educational programs and public policies (U.S. Department of Education, 2012). Parents are also a stakeholder sector, serving as first models and educators for their offspring; they are also informed and passionate civic advocates on behalf of their families (Jenkins, 2009). As another professional example, psychologists study the psychological aspects of social issues such as the impact of fake news, train clientele and advocate on their behalf relative to social services such as education and health, respond to needs of the public relative to civic issues, and participate in civic issues such as conflict prevention and resolution (American Psychological Association, 2020).

Youth are unique stakeholders in civic engagement as their lives are controlled by adult-determined laws, resources and practices. Youth have no voting rights so may feel marginalized. Many youths are socially minded, but it is often hard for them to articulate their ideas or to be taken seriously, especially amid the din of communication. In studying practices that cultivate youth engagement, Generation Citizen (2019) found that new adults (in their 20s and 30s) participated little in politics and had little civic knowledge, especially among Blacks, Latinx, English language learners, low SES individuals, and offspring of parents with little civic engagement. Furthermore, under-served populations tended to do collective action such as demonstrating rather than voting, because they lacked civic resources and were civically disillusioned. Nevertheless, early introduction to civic engagement helps youth develop positive developmental outcomes and predicts the degree of adult civic engagement (Middaugh, Clark & Ballard, 2017). In terms of fake news, youth are particularly vulnerable because they have less knowledge and experience than adults to draw upon in order to discern fake news. Furthermore, as active social media users, youth are likely to share and spread fake news as a way to belong socially or gain social status. Youth may well be the greatest victims of fake news, especially if they feel that they have no agency.

Conditions for civic engagement

Several conditions need to be in place for effective civic engagement. Youth.gov (2020) identified four constructs that are needed for civic engagement at any age: civic commitment, civic skills, social cohesion and civic action. Some factors are internal such as motivation and commitment. Some conditions such as knowledge and skills need to be internally integrated, but need to be introduced and explained within learning environments. Still other conditions focus on communication: communication tools such as technologies and the civic space within which to communicate. When these conditions are in place, and people have opportunities to gain and apply expertise, they develop social empowerment and can make a difference civically.

Personal conditions

Civic engagement integrates cognitive, emotional and behavioral components (Bobek et al., 2009), which shape personal identity. Individuals' personalities reflect basic nature and nurturing. Individuals' background and experiences influence their development of attitudes, values, cognition and interests. Cognitive processes and motivations intertwine with behaviors, which are contextually situated within one's environment. How individuals react and interact socially within those environments and situations also shape their civic engagement. It should be noted that individuals are both internally and externally motivated, so that civic engagement, such as addressing fake news, may be instigated externally because of social incentives, but the motivation – and sustained civic engagement – may become internalized.

Individuals' civic knowledge and skills develop through engagement with their environment, largely through interacting with people and material resources. Some learning is experiential, such as trial-and-error reactions to stimuli (such as consequences of fighting). Functional literacy, in contrast, requires explicit training, which is a basis for self-learning through recorded information. Formal and informal education attempts to facilitate learning and practice, including how to think critically and learn purposefully. In any case, though, the onus is on the individual to choose to engage and change behavior; that choice applies to dealing with fake news as well.

Communication skills

Civic engagement requires communication skills, largely through language. While people are usually comfortable communicating in social situations, fewer are adept in public civic discourse (Bennett, Wells & Rank, 2009). Many online discussion forums tend to assert personal opinions more than promote respectful and deep deliberation. Those opinions are more likely than well-researched evidence, which makes them more susceptible to fake news.

Giroux (2005) asserted that education offers tools for systematic critique of power and social contexts, and language for creating democratic change. However, most civics classes focus on teaching government basics and encourage students to follow political events, but they do not provide opportunities for students to self-express their opinions in the public arena and engage in thoughtful civic deliberations. Since many youths use social media, educators can build on teens' interests by linking them to similarly-minded websites to help them reach relevant civic decision-makers, thereby offering a higher profile for civic action such as countering fake news (Bennett, 2008). At the same time, individuals need to gain media literacy so they can leverage the key features of each medium to communicate their message in the most effective way in light of their target audience (Jenkins, 2009).

Communication skills also involve the ability to collaborate and network (Jenkins, 2009). In working in groups, individuals need to identify effective roles for themselves and ways that they can contribute to mutual goals. Individuals need to be able to pool knowledge to form collective intelligence as well as negotiate conflicting information and meaning in order to form a coherent plan of action. These skills are particularly important as spreading fake news can be a way to maintain social ties, but it can also jeopardize long-term trust; collective intelligence can foster critical thinking that can stop fake news spread and disperse accurate thoughtful news instead. Social media offers an effective communications channel to gain and practice these important communication skills in a community. For instance, in Spain, Twitter mobilized and organized collective protests against privatizing public services (Saura et al., 2017).

Civic space

People need to have venues in order to express and share ideas. Interaction between government agencies and citizens builds a sense of community, participation and interdependence. A public civic space provides a means for government agencies to inform citizens so that those agencies can operate more effectively. Likewise, to be effective and responsive, governments need to know their citizens: their potential, their contributions to society, their needs and their concerns. Even if citizens disagree with the government, offering a public space to air those perspectives enables governments to identify and monitor potential problems. All parties should be respected and held accountable for such venues to succeed.

One significant type of civic space is affinity space (Jenkins, 2009) where people can gather informally to share interests and respond to short-term needs flexibly. Such spaces allow for easy movement and low barriers for membership flow. Their loose structure also facilitates innovation and shared empowerment.

Ideally, civic space should consist of a coordinated set of communication channels: convenient and dependable face-to-face town halls and other gathering areas, telecommunications, public and privately-owned media outlets, formal and informal educational institutions, public and private agencies and organizations, and workplace settings. Citizens should be able to access and communicate information via those channels through text, image and sound.

At this point in time, online provision and exchange of information is a necessary condition, especially as so much information is now created, stored and retrieved only in digital form (OECD, 2003). This condition thus requires that all citizens have physical and intellectual access to online information. Governments need to provide telecommunications (including the Internet) infrastructures and ensure that they are maintained and supported. Citizens need physical access to online information, including stable Internet-connected devices and digital channels. They also need training in accessing and using online resources, which includes technical skills to operate those devices. Those Internet service providers also have civic space responsibilities: dependable and equitable access and support, data security, provisions for privacy, and compliance with legal regulations such as accommodations for individuals with disabilities.

Technology

Technology facilitates civic engagement because it offers more varied and convenient ways to access, analyze, communicate with, and contribute to civic organizations and their information. Potentially, technology-based media can expose people to different ideas that can promote deeper understanding and appreciation of various views, and lead to greater belief in democracy and civic engagement. On the other hand, with more media channels that offer narrow broadcasting, individuals can easily stay in their information bubble, and become more polarized than ever. More specifically, technology impacts fake news, which in turn impacts civic engagement. At the same time that technology can significantly expand access to news, it can also "flatten" it such that it is harder for audiences to discern the relative importance of news stories. Without digital literacy, people can be misled by false information and lose trust in both the media and politics, which can dampen civic engagement. Thus, knowledge of technology's impact on fake news can help inform individuals – and foster their own civic voice and action.

Technological advances and the rise of social media have lowered the entry barriers for accessing, generating and sharing information, including action for social causes. Indeed, social media may be participatory media, offering a vibrant virtual environment of public discourse (Bohman, 2004). That same ease of access, unfortunately, also enables people to create and spread fake news. Therefore, people need digital skills, along with cognitive and communication expertise, to optimize their online presence to effect social change.

At the same time that technology can offer venues for disenfranchised people to have more voice for civic engagement, technology can also reveal deeper issues of information inequity, which needs to be addressed as part of civic action. For instance, Lievrouw and Farb (2003) recognized the relationship between information and social equity. They considered information as an intangible public good, yet those people with greater social and economic power have greater physical and intellectual access to information and are more likely to generate, shape and disseminate information. To counteract this inequality requires civic reform – and civic engagement. Lievrouw and Farb recommended establishing information policies for access that ensure even distribution of information resources and learning opportunities to gain information and civic competency.

Civic engagement challenges

Even with social empowerment, individuals face challenges in engaging civically. Information in general, and specifically with regard to fake news, is a key factor. Its issues have been addressed already: who creates fake news and why, the viral spread of fake news, access to fake news, filter bubbles that screen conflicting information, lack of comprehension of information in a foreign language, the lack of literacies to discern and analyze fake news, and the lack of information and knowledge to compare and counter fake news.

Time is another subtle challenge throughout the news communication cycle. Journalists are under increasingly short deadlines, so they do not always verify news sources or wait until all the information is uncovered to publish a news story (Rubin, 2019). People may feel overwhelmed by the barrage of news, and not feel there is time enough to cull through all the noise to find a grain of truth and then act on it (Mukerjee, 2017). People may have job and family demands that eat up their time, leaving them with little time to participate civically. Time can also impact interest; people may pay attention to social issues during election campaign periods but their interest might wane after the election when other events gain high profile; as a result, civic engagement may be hard to sustain (Levy, Solomon & Collet-Gildard, 2016). Especially as some societal issues are not easy fixes, and take much time and effort to solve, all but the most persistent people can become frustrated and demoralized.

Civic engagement also runs up against attitudes of distrust, frustration, weariness, fear and despair. For instance, when people distrust the media, the government and other public institutions, they may withdraw from civic engagement. When people think that their opinion does not count or that there is no chance of change, they may despair or give up. In a dictatorship, people may fear that civic engagement will lead to personal or familial danger. Attitudes can also affect which social causes to pursue. For instance, Pinazo-Calatayud, Nos-Aldas and Agut-Nieto (2020) found that people were more motivated to act when the messages they received were more negative to their cause. When examining the factors for civic disengagement during a violent Mexican election period, Drs. Grijalva-Verdugo and Moreno-Candil (2017) discovered that media literacy was not the main factor; weariness and distrust of political institutions was the root factor. The researchers stated that urgency of social empowerment through knowledge bonding contributed to concrete civic action against the national violence.

The Organisation for Economic Co-operation and Development (OECD) identified five challenges for online civic engagement in 2003, and these challenges continue to persist.

- Capacity. How can individuals gain and practice policy-making skills?
- Scale. Can governments listen to, evaluate and address the increasing number of civic voices?
- Commitment. Are governments committed to analyzing and using civic input? How can governments be held accountable to such processes?
- Coherence. How can governments leverage technology to establish more coherent and transparent systems to address social issues and develop effective policies that include citizen participation?
- Evaluation. How can the effectiveness of online civic engagement be measured and evaluated?

Civics education

At this point, the importance of civics education is a critical factor for civic engagement, be it political or not. In 2017 the OECD asserted that the process of civics education affects individuals' beliefs, commitment, abilities and actions as community members. Civics education fosters civic knowledge and skills, it improves attitudes toward public and political institutions, it promotes civic equality, it facilitates social empowerment, and it leads to greater civic engagement effectiveness. As it relates to fake news, civics education encourages and informs news consumption and production. Nevertheless, similar to civic engagement in general, civics education also encounters challenges: ensuring high-quality curriculum when governments do not prioritize such knowledge, inequitable instruction to marginalized populations, lack of funding for instruction, and polarized political climate where curriculum change may be perceived as a political agenda more than as a public good (Guilfoile & Delander, 2014).

Curriculum

Civics education does not include a universal curriculum; it is likely to be shaped by cultural and political values and realities. Hence, according to Gould (2011), citizen education curriculum and co-curriculum may consist of several different frameworks.

- History curriculum: studying social and political history and accompanying significant documents such as constitutions.
- Government/civics curriculum: studying the structure and processes of government, its laws, and politics.
- Critical thinking: active evaluation and analysis of content and issues.
- Community service: volunteer work at community agencies.
- Service learning: community service that applies academic curriculum, usually with the intent to identify and solve community issues.
- Voter training: studying electoral issues and voting processes.

While several frameworks exist, most of them address the rights and responsibilities of citizens and their community in terms of knowledge, skills and dispositions. In examining civics education curriculum around the world, the OECD (2017) found that civics education concepts usually include human rights, politico-institutional arrangements and electoral processes. UNESCO (2015) parsed the domains of civic learning into cognitive (knowledge about societal issues and critical thinking), social-emotional (sense of belonging, empathy, solidarity and respect), and behavioral aspects (action for peace and sustainability). Krahanbuhl (2017) positioned civics education domains in classic terms: grammar (knowledge), logic (critical thinking) and rhetoric (action of persuasion). The Center for Civic Education (Branson, 1998) identified three general foci: civic knowledge, civic skills of critical thinking and methods of participation, and civic dispositions that support democracy. The Council of Europe (2016) detailed those strands, and subdivided disposition into attitudes and values.

- Knowledge and critical understanding of self, language and communication, and the world.
- Skills of listening and observing, analysis, lifelong learning, empathy, flexibility and adaptability, linguistics, cooperation and conflict resolution.
- Attitudes of responsibility, self-efficacy, openness, respect, civic-mindedness, tolerance of ambiguity.
- Value human dignity and rights, cultural diversity, democracy, justice and fairness, equality and rule of law.

The 2016 International Association for the Evaluation of Education Achievement (IEA) posited a similar framework for civic and citizenship education: of content knowledge, cognitive process, and behavior. IEA then contextualized this framework within school community characteristics and perceptions as well as the wider community's characteristics and relationships with education.

Schulz et al. (2016) also identified new issues in civics education: globalization and diversity, environmental sustainability, morality, and social media. Increasingly now, to that list can be public health issues. Particularly with greater incorporation of technology into civic activity, the concept of eCitizenship and supportive curriculum has emerged. For instance, OECD (2017) discovered that media use and information-seeking behavior predicts greater civic learning and participation. As such, individuals need to research, assess and use information sources as they engage in online public discourse so that they can develop informed and critical perspectives as well as build networks of civic mobilization. Middaugh, Clark and Ballard (2017) echoed the need for digital skills, especially as digital tools play an important part of youth development. Young people's online communication and media products foster civic engagement.

Kahne, Hodgin and Eidman-Aadahl (2016) pushed the civics education envelope even further, using digital age participatory politics as the pivot point. They asserted that civic and political engagement practices need to be taught differently because those practices are enacted differently and in different contexts. Black Lives Matter, the DREAMer movement, responses to mass shootings, and a global climate movement are being led by youth advocates who leverage social networks and street demonstrations for social justice and reform. As noted above, learners need to gain competency in four core practices of participatory politics. To that end, learners need to utilize the affordances of digital tools for gathering data and researching, hone critical thinking skills to evaluate information, engage effectively with audiences, develop more sophisticated production and communication skills, and polish political practices.

Having a solid civics education curriculum in place is crucial, but there is no guarantee that effective teaching and learning will occur. Schulz et al. (2016) asserted that civics education varies because of student characteristics and expectations, instructional design and implementation, and the context in which this curriculum is delivered. Nevertheless, several research-based practices can lead to more effective learning. For instance, most studies encourage civics education across the curriculum as well as in co-curricular activities for extended periods of time. Classes should discuss current issues, especially those suggested by the students, in an open-minded climate. These discussions offer students opportunities to acquire and practice public discourse skills such as interpretation, respectful but polemic debate, in-depth cross-examination of ideas, and student-led action research (Generation Citizen, 2019; OECD, 2017). Schulz et al. (2016) suggested some good websites to facilitate such discussions: www.crf-use.org/deliberating-in-a-democracy/deliberating-in-a-democracy.html, www.mlkvachallenge.org and www.facinghistory.org/. Students should also have opportunities to practice civic skills in school, such as participating in student government and clubs, and creating student publications such as newspapers and public service announcements. Furthermore, schools should partner with community entities to facilitate students' service learning, which benefits both academic learning and civic commitment; examples include local media outlets, public and non-profit organizations, service clubs such as Rotary and Lions, youth-serving organizations, and local civic projects.

Orth and Chen (2013) encouraged educators to partner with families to provide citizen education, especially since parents are responsible for their children's digital and civic life outside of school. Orth and Chen outlined a citizen education program as follows.

1. Create a shared vision of the citizen education program, and identify desired student learning outcomes, methods of integration into the existing curriculum, relevant and available resources, people responsible for implementation, and alignment with school policies.
2. Train teachers and engage parents. Establish an online repository of courses that are accessible by the entire school community.
3. Implement the program. Establish an advisory group, and build in benchmarks for assessment and adjustments. Identify student peer leaders to model and discuss civic behavior issues.

While few civics education frameworks or curricula explicitly address fake news, their content and activities certainly inform learners as they encounter and deal with fake news. In addition, fake news can serve as a critical lens with which to approach civic concepts such as critical evaluation of information, rhetorical strategies, and civic-related social media use. Furthermore, knowledge of fake news can help youth with community-based service learning such as citizen science.

Civics education learning activities

The following list offers curricula to help educators teach civic literacy.

- American Political Science Association – Civic education and engagement: www. apsanet.org/RESOURCES/For-Faculty/Civic-Education-amp-Engagement
- Baylor University – How to teach civics in action to K-12 students: https:// onlinegrad.baylor.edu/resources/teaching-civic-education-democracy/
- Chicago Public Schools Social Science and Civic Engagement: https://cps. edu/Pages/socialsciencecivicengagement.aspx
- Generation Citizen: https://generationcitizen.org/our-programs/our-curric ulum/

Community-based civic engagement

Civics education and practice also occur outside the parameters of formal education (Cho, Byrne & Aelter, 2020). Affinity groups can thrive in many physical and virtual environments. In some cases, local specificity of civic concerns can be more meaningful for individuals because they can see the difference that their contribution makes; local efforts can also facilitate social bonding that complements civic action. Community-based civic engagement can also promote and support civics education and the development of digital literacy. Especially when community groups appreciate individuals' creations of varied content that advances their agenda, such as combating fake news, those creators gain self-esteem and well-being.

Sometimes the fault for youth reluctance to engage civically lies with adults, who often overlook youth's perspective when making policy and political decisions. Frustrated or cynical about politicians' ineffectiveness of bringing about change, many youths prefer to focus on single issues such as pollution or human trafficking. Recognizing cause-related enthusiasm, radical groups do see the potential of youth to act on their behalf. Such groups manipulate social media to spread disinformation, including fake news and false glamour, to attract and recruit youth to their own radical causes (Barrett, 2018; UN Department of Economic and Social Affairs, 2016).

Fortunately, governments are starting to integrate youth into civic action. The governments of Jordan, Morocco and Tunisia have all reached out to the maximum number of stakeholders, including youth, through social media in order to hear everyone's voices and share civic responsibilities (OECD, 2018). To optimize results, these governments coordinate youth-informed policies across ministries, working centrally and locally. The organization of youth engagement varies in different locales; formats include youth councils, youth parliaments, advisory committees and youth campaigns. To build youth capacity, local youth centers give youth responsibility and autonomy, space and Internet channels for information gathering and exchanging information, and a base for solidarity. Open government tools and mechanisms also support youth engagement and visibility. As a result, youth are consulted when formulating policy and designing services, they participate in budget decisions, and they assess the impact of laws on youth in general.

Digital citizenship

Civic engagement, even if focused only on addressing fake news, can take many forms, both physical and virtual. However, since so many people access news digitally, it makes sense to include digital citizenship when discussing civic engagement. Digital citizenship not only addresses responsible technology usage, but also encourages leveraging technology to foster civic engagement (Wells, 2015).

Definitions

Digital citizenship is a term used to define the appropriate and responsible use of technology among users. Digital citizenship basically consists of the ability to use technology safely, critically, productively, responsively and civically. For individuals to use technology productively, they need digital literacy and information literacy. It should be noted that digital literacy for citizens differs in that it addresses a whole range of digital concepts and skills, but does not necessarily deal explicitly with pro-active civic engagement. More often, digital citizenship focuses on the legal and ethical dimension of technology. The 2016 ISTE standards for students stated that digital citizens "recognize the rights, responsibilities and opportunities of living, learning and working in an interconnected digital world, and they act and model in ways that are safe, legal and ethical" (p. 1). Practices include managing personal data and digital identities, respecting intellectual property, and interacting online appropriately. It should be recognized that digital citizenship does not explicitly define "community," particularly as virtual communities can sometimes play a more meaningful role in a person's life than a physical neighborhood. The world's borders are potentially very porous.

Models and standards

Just as there are several variations in defining digital citizenship, several models of digital citizenship exist in government, non-profit organizations and private sectors. It should be noted that many digital literacy standards, such as UNESCO's and ISTE's, embed digital citizenship rather than develop a separate set of standards, which has merit. No matter the type of literacy, one should practice that literacy responsibly and ethically.

In 2015 UNESCO Bangkok synthesized key elements of digital citizenship based on governmental, non-governmental organizational and private sector responses. Those elements included: benefits of ICT (information and communication technology) use and online participation, responsible and ethical behavior, safety and protection against risks, and values reinforcement (i.e., respect, empathy, etc.). Their report includes several Asian and Oceanian digital citizenship frameworks. Similarly, the Council of Europe (Frau-Meigs et al., 2017) analyzed European countries' digital citizenship models, which are found in their report.

In synthesizing existing research on digital citizenship, Moonsun Choi (2016) identified four interrelated digital citizenship categories: ethics, media and information literacy, participation and engagement, and critical resistance.

Probably the most popular digital citizenship model in the U.S. was developed by Mike Ribble (2015). He identified nine elements clustered into three principles.

- Respect, which encompasses digital access, digital law and digital etiquette.
- Educate, which encompasses digital literacy, digital communication and digital commerce knowledge.
- Protect, which encompasses digital rights and responsibilities such as free speech and privacy, digital security, and health.

Lindsay and Davis (2012) developed the enlightened digital citizenship model, which focuses on technical awareness on several levels: individual, social, cultural and global. Intersecting and relating to awareness are four rays of understanding: literacy and fluency; habits of learning; etiquette and respect; and safety, privacy, copyright and legal aspects.

Parekh's 2003 digital citizenship model extended to a global orientation, which has three elements: examining and questioning one's own country and its policies, active interest in other countries' affairs, and commitment to create a just world order.

Even at the civic engagement level of personal responsibility, digital citizenship can be applied when analyzing the digital ethical responsibilities and practices of other people, such as political groups and news organizations. However, digital citizenship has even more impact at the higher levels of civic engagement, when citizens can combat digital fake news as a social justice cause.

Digital citizenship education

The above digital citizenship definitions, models and standards can form the basis for digital citizenship education and shape instructional design. However, such action assumes teacher knowledge of – and skill in – digital citizenship, along with the ability to design and deliver instruction for effective learning and application. Those assumptions have been tested and often found wanting.

In examining the research about the beliefs, preparation and practices of teachers relative to digital citizenship education, Walters, Gee and Mohammed (2019) found that most teachers held narrow definitions of digital citizenship. While they thought that those aspects were important, a gap existed between those positive attitudes and what teachers are doing to implement digital citizenship into their instruction, especially in elementary school settings. The field is so new that many teachers do not feel well-prepared and competent to create and deliver such curriculum, and even teacher preparation programs tend to tread lightly in this area, usually focusing on safe and responsible digital professional use, which they can model in the classroom. However, few teacher preparation programs go the extra step to address how to teach digital citizenship to others, let alone promote pro-active civic engagement through technology (Armfield & Blocher, 2019; Walters, Gee & Mohammed, 2019). In practice, teachers or librarians are more likely to provide a one-shot session on digital safety and intellectual property compliance. Especially in elementary education, teachers often rely on "canned" commercial digital citizenship units, offered in a vacuum, separated from the rest of the school's curriculum (Walters, Gee & Mohammed, 2019). Even civics courses seldom address the digital nature of civics and its ethical aspects, nor use digital tools responsibly for civic engagement. That confluence of elements is largely missing.

Nevertheless, researchers and policy-makers have made valuable recommendations about digital citizenship curriculum. For instance, UNESCO has several resources for digital citizenship education (https://en.unesco.org/sites/default/files/sru-ict_mapping_report_2014.pdf). Most experts assert that digital citizenship education should be embedded across the curriculum and started as early as primary school (Frau-Meigs et al., 2017; Hollandsworth, Donovan & Welch, 2017; UNESCO, 2015; U.S. Department of Education, 2012). Their rationale is that digital citizenship informs critical thinking skills and communication skills, which are manifested in different ways for different subjects. For instance, multimodal approaches to public writing can lead to learner public civic discourse and advocacy (Warren-Riley & Hurley, 2017). In contrast, technology has facilitated science investigations – and the manipulation of data, so learners need to understand the digital ethics of scientific methods (Senabre, Ferran-Ferrer & Perello, 2018).

Furthermore, digital citizenship is most effective when addressed explicitly with authentic and meaningful tasks that motivate and activate learners. When teaching and promoting digital citizenship, formal and informal educators need to make learners aware of digital citizenship issues, engage learners in grappling with those issues, and guide learners in ways to solve those issues both within and beyond the school community (Frau-Meigs et al., 2017). Taking fake news as an example, educators can survey their students about their knowledge and perceptions of fake news, which can serve as a diagnostic tool to identify digital literacy and citizenship gaps. Educators can share examples about fake news and its possible dire consequences such as Pizzagate and disease, aiming for issues that personally connect with those students. These examples can then lead to analysis of those fake news stories: point of view, connotative and emotional words and images, manipulation of images, comparison with other sources about the same news, etc. This process can also incentivize honing research skills. With this new information, students are poised to take action civically, such as countering fake news online or teaching others how to discern fake news.

In the process of teaching digital citizenship, Diez-Gutierrez and Diaz-Nafria (2018) asserted the need for incorporating soft skills such as empathy, social cooperation, and the ability to meet cognitive and social challenges. Such skills are particularly relevant when tying digital citizenship to civic engagement. The researchers cautioned that such expanded learning needs to be actively supported by teachers in the form of an open, democratic and collaborative learning environment.

It should also be recognized that for digital citizenship education to happen, educators must ensure that digital platforms, including social media, are inclusive and available to all. Educations also need to make sure that learners gain intellectual access to technology. Furthermore, access to content itself should be developmentally appropriate, yet not biased against difficult dialogues nor likely to create echo chambers where learners have little exposure to different views. These factors can also serve as teaching moments for learners to become aware of digital inequities and to consider ways to address those inequities so that all individuals can participate in their communities (Floridi, 2010).

Lastly, it is not enough to practice digital citizenship academically. Gleason and von Gillern (2018) stipulated that teachers need to provide opportunities for learners to apply digital citizenship through out-of-school civic engagement. To that end, the authors recommended incorporating social media into instruction that leverages students' daily online experiences and validates learners' social online interests as a way to empower them to improve their communities, be they local or virtual. Such responsible digital civic action also publicly validates learners' ability to engage civically in an authentic and significant way. Some student-empowering activities that enable learners to apply digital citizenship skills for civic engagement include creating digital products for the community, recording community events as well as capturing oral and visual history, and training community members in responsible digital use – including the discernment of – and reaction to – fake news.

News-related community-based civic engagement examples

Increasingly, people participate and interact through social networks to influence political action (McGrew et al., 2017). They can serve as a collective intelligence to solve complex, knotty social problems. To combat fake news, for instance, individuals can participate in citizen science and journalism. They can also deal with fake news creatively through art activism. Especially as people understand how fake news can impact their own meaningful contexts, they may be motivated to get engaged civically.

Action research

As mentioned above, community-based action research offers a meaningful way to engage civically. Individuals and groups identify personally important areas for local improvement, gather data about the situation, analyze those data, make recommendations for ways to address the situation, and then develop and implement concrete action plans to improve the community. When formal education facilitates an authentic bridge between the school community and the community at large, students learn from knowledgeable adults in both settings and gain both academic and social capital. In reviewing civic education and youth development literacy efforts, the National Action Civics Collaborative identified key learning outcomes of action research: civic and cultural transformation, informed and engaged citizenship, civic creation, and positive youth leadership (Gingold, 2013). To achieve these outcomes, learners need the following competencies: civic knowledge, civic values, critical thinking, communication, collaboration, agency, professionalism, and general academic skills. In several cases, students can learn those competences by hands-on activity, which makes that learning even more meaningful.

Action research may be applied to fake news in that participants can gather in-the-field data about community knowledge and use of fake news, and then explore the consequences of such use, such as political voting or health decisions. The action researchers can analyze those data and develop counter measures to mitigate those decisions, from providing alternative bases for decision-making or teaching how to discern fake news in the first place.

Citizen journalism

Most journalists model civic engagement: gaining insights into the conditions of their community and informing their public to facilitate societal improvement. Increasingly, journalists realize the importance of community engagement in collecting news. Especially as special interest groups or traditionally underrepresented groups have insider information that mainstream journalists have little access to or understanding of, media outlets realize the importance of inclusive and diverse voices and perspectives. In that respect, journalists' roles have changed to some degree, focusing more on developing relationships with their community and curating contributed news. Such actions can lead to citizen journalism: both user-centered news production and participatory journalism bias (Siapera & Veglis, 2012).

Journalism has also become more professional in nature, and specialized training is now the norm. As noted before, journalists have also adopted codes of ethics to guide their practice. As journalists work with their community contributors, they also see the importance of educating those contributors as to journalistic processes and skills. By such education and training, journalists hope to gather higher-quality credible news contributions and greater community trust. Furthermore, with the advent of social media, including for news dissemination, the barriers for participation have significantly lowered.

Citizen journalism holds special promise for young people: as a way to voice the issues that are important to them, as a concrete way to engage civically, and as a means of career exploration. By collecting and disseminating news about community concerns and collaborating with media outlets, teens can act as social agents and see themselves as contributors for societal development (Dahlgren, 2005). Furthermore, youth respond well when given responsibilities to serve their communities, which leads to more positive personal development (Bennett, 2008).

Both formal and informal education offers valuable opportunities for young people to gain the knowledge and skills of public discourse through journalistic service learning. Student publications have a long history, but active partnerships with local news outlets is less traditional. Probably the most common area of collaboration historically has been sports, with student reporters and videographers of high school games. However, misperceptions and even fake news about youth and other marginalized groups offers a window of opportunity for those populations to correct those misperceptions and possible fake news in a range of topics. As an example, to sustain non-profit, inclusive journalism, Community Partners (2020) created several projects to empower under-served communities. For instance, they partnered with USC, LA Times and PCC to train high schoolers to combat fake news. They taught the youths how to fact-check and write without bias as those skills gave them opportunities to pitch news stories and get published. One of their news hubs, Youthwire, produces publications in partnerships with local newspapers; the writers consist of teens and new adults who are largely people of color.

Journalism departments in post-secondary institutions routinely encourage students to do service learning or do internships at local media outlets, which is particularly valuable in a world of fake news. These offerings are not limited to pre-professional journalists but also to other majors, who can leverage their subject expertise such as political science or sociology to gather news from inside sources and analyze news, including fake news, using the critical lens of the academic domain. This emerging practice has been called a "teaching hospital" model because it mirrors how physicians are trained. Another civic-minded model is entrepreneurial in which students with journalism training work with non-traditional news outlets. In either case, the focus is on civic engagement through citizen journalism: fact-finding and truth-telling through the fifth estate (Fleming, 2017).

On the other hand, many people have been excluded from academia, but social media has enabled them to access venues for communication that they never had before. For example, in Spain, media outlets have prioritized citizen agendas and sources. Journalists have also educated the populous to participate civically through communication processes. News organizations have also provided technical support and facilitated social skills to motivate participants and give them more self-confidence as they contribute to those news outlets, including countering fake news (Lema-Blanco, Rodriguez-Gomez & Barranquero-Carretero, 2016).

Citizen science

Another significant source of fake news is pseudo-science, which has berated global warming, COVID-19, and even evolution. Some fake news occurs because of insufficient testing, misrepresented or "doctored" data, misleading interpretation of the data, lack of peer review to verify the research, as well as cherry-picking existing studies to advance the communicator's agenda (Peters et al., 2018). Science education needs more emphasis to be sure, and science itself needs continuous oversight, but bots that spread fake news and filter bubbles exacerbate the situation when people do not encounter other perspectives. In addition, scientists tend to publish in scholarly journals for their peers, and tend not to use layman's terms in those few cases that they publish in popular magazines. The disconnect between scientists and the general public helps no one (Hunter, 2016). Fortunately, scientists are now trying to reach out to the public, not only to inform them but also to engage them in scientific initiatives. For instance, extensive science communication training and consolidation have occurred in Portugal, and the country's marine scientists are researching out to audiences to support public engagement activities (Pinto, Costa & Cabral, 2018). With the outbreak of COVID-19, several scientific crowdsourcing projects want citizen involvement to track the virus (www.citizenscience.org/covid-19/).

Concurrently, the Open Science movement has pushed for more transparent research and more open exchange of information. This movement also entails use of new technologies and citizen participation. Such citizen sciences can get involved throughout the science project: from forming research questions, recording and analyzing observations, and acting on the findings (Senabre, Ferran-Ferrer & Perello, 2018). The most common civic engagement in science is data collection in which people in different locales measure specific scientific data, such as weather or pollution, and send it to a centralized data collection site for analysis. Such participation facilitates scientific recommendations as well as producing a community of participants who feel a sense of consequential community (Peters & Besley, 2019).

At least two categories of citizen science have emerged (G7 Science Academies, 2019). Community-based participatory research consists of partnerships between professional researchers and citizens, mainly to collect data. Biodiversity, medicine and weather conditions are particularly popular projects. Another category is called "beyond the walls" research, which is usually conducted by scientists outside the walls of academia, government or industry. Such scientists may collaborate on special commissions or start-up projects, or they may conduct "do it yourself" projects in small groups or individually.

To guide science practitioners, both professional and amateur, the European Citizen Science Association (2015) developed ten principles of citizen science. These principles can also be applied to combat fake news that might arrive in scientific communication, as noted in italics.

- Citizen science projects actively involve people to advance understanding or knowledge. *Participants learn accurate scientific methods that provide evidence for truthful stances.*
- Citizen science projects have genuine science outcomes. *Projects aim for impactful results that advance knowledge and society.*
- Citizen scientists may participate at various points in the scientific process. *Participants learn that each step in the scientific method has ethical considerations.*
- Citizen sciences get feedback from projects. *Participants should be notified if their actions are not ethical or accurate so they can rectify their actions.*
- Citizen science considers and controls biases and limitations. *Participants should be aware of their own biases and try to overcome them in the science process.*
- Citizen science projects and their results are made publicly available, when appropriate. *Participants should be aware that their projects will have public scrutiny and must have trustworthy content. On the positive side, publication informs the public and facilitates societal improvement.*
- Citizen sciences are acknowledged by projects appropriately. *Participants should expect fair and transparent public attribution; this action helps the public to trust science.*
- Citizen science programs should be considered in terms of their outcomes and benefits when evaluated. *Participants should conduct themselves knowledgeably and ethically throughout their effort. Their quality work can help promote more citizen science.*
- Citizen science project leaders should consider ethical and legal aspects of their work. *Participants should expect that their project leaders will maintain ethical and legal standards, and will provide training and oversight to ensure such compliance.*

In the non-profit sector, National Geographic Society has a relatively long history of engaging in crowdsourced data gathering, and has expanded the role of their constituents to participants meaningfully in their scientific efforts. For example, National Geographic has now developed a National Geographic Young Explorer program, which funds innovative fieldwork to new adults. The April issue of *National Geographic* (Parker, 2020) featured several of these explorers and other young civic activists whose projects focus on life on earth. Green Hope Foundation, founded by teenager Kehkashan Basu, uses environment academics to empower youth to deal with climate change, land degradation, biodiversity conservation and clean energy. Groups have planted thousands of trees and created solar lamps for clean energy. As a preteen, Felix Finkbeiner founded a tree-planting non-profit organization, which offers workshops to teach children about global warming so they can become climate justice ambassadors. Teenager Delaney Reynolds founded the Sink or Swim Project to educate people about the risks of sea-level rise, and encourage them to solve that problem.

It should be recognized, though, that citizen scientists themselves can be engaged in research misconduct, which may lead to fake news being broadcast. With mainstream science under public scrutiny, scientists have heightened their own regulations and reviews, which are harder to enforce with decentralized data gathering and processing. However, the principal investigators are, ultimately, the ones held accountable, and their own careers and reputations are at stake. The consequences might also include further deterioration of trust in science. While such citizen scientists could be held liable for misconduct, such cases could be hard to prove and would certainly be time-consuming. Peer review offers a reasonable front-end approach to the problem; if reviewers question the study, the original authors can confront misguided citizens and provide the necessary training to hone skills – and supervise the work carefully to ensure quality control, discuss the ethical ramifications of science, or ultimately retract the data and the person's participation. Ideally, these measures should be implemented before the study even begins in order to communicate clear expectations, and then spot-check early in the process so timely interventions can be done. Rasmussen (2019) also suggested considering a research integrity insurance agreement whereby the citizen scientists would pay a nominal fee to state that they hold themselves accountable to the researchers or to a professional organization; the fees would be used to support the costs of possible ethical inquiry. As Rasmussen concluded, if citizen science cannot be trusted, then that kind of participation cannot be used, which decreases the number of data points, makes the research less generalizable, and lessens public civic engagement.

On the other hand, citizen scientists can also rout out fake news in science or pseudo-science, as exemplified in sociologist Nick Adam's course (Todd, 2018). His students dissect science news stories in terms of the entire science process. Their analyses are shared on *PublicEditor* (https://goodlylabs.org/pe.html), which assesses popular news articles, and assigns them a credibility score and badge. Technically, citizen scientists could expand their critical eyes even earlier in the research process, thus providing another check-and-balance in scientific endeavors and ultimately raise public trust.

Arts activism

Arts as civic engagement and arts activism has both a short and long history. Goya's "The Disasters of War," Daumier's political cartoons, Kathe Kollwitz's charcoal drawings of war and poverty, Diego Rivera's murals, Picasso's "Guernica," Cindy Sherman's feminist photographs all exemplify compelling visual social commentary. Likewise, performing arts such as music, dance and theater have a long history, from Aristophanes' "The Birds" and Shakespeare's "Macbeth" to the 1930s' "The Cradle Will Rock," the 1960s' "Hair," and the 1990s' "Rent." Likewise, protest songs have existed for centuries, from "The Marseilles" anthem and African spirituals to WWII's "Bella Ciao" anti-Vietnam rock-and-roll; even the Broadway song "Do you hear the people sing" became an anthem in the 2019 Hong Kong protests. Activist and protest arts are generally considered a 20th century phenomena, but they have gained more ground in the last 50 years. Technology has significantly expanded the artistic tools available and the means to access and broadcast artistic expressions. These examples express a range of civic engagement, from taking a community art class or acting in local theater to gain socially-inclusive artistic appreciation and knowledge, to expressing strong opinions and motivating people to address social issues such as fake news (Stern & Seifert, 2009).

Today, arts civic engagement and activism exists around the world. In India, grassroots feminist groups reinterpreted folk dance as street theater to express concerns about rape, inheritance law, and women's representation in texts (Garlough, 2008). Refugees in Germany have formed and leveraged their political identities to use performative exercise for German audiences as a means of demonstrating their struggles and counter injustices that they have faced (Bhimji, 2016). Both in North America and across national borders, women have reclaimed and celebrated the feminized craft of knitting, and leveraged it as a means to build community and incorporate their practice as a political tool to dialogue about gendered roles, unequal distribution of wealth, class, and ability (Pentney, 2008). The book *The Aesthetics of Global Protest* (McGarry et al., 2020) collected stories from around the world that showcase art activism: queer visual activism in South Africa; political street art in Argentina, Istanbul and Athens; photography and protest in Israel and Palestine; music videos as protest communication in Turkey. As a study by the James Foundation revealed (Rabkin, 2017), people who participate civically in the arts tend to volunteer and exhibit social tolerance. Furthermore, those participants often credit community-based arts experience as significant for their personal development and identity.

Several artistic groups have addressed misleading information and fake news head on. The True False Film Festival uses documentaries to explore social issues and approaches. Australian street theater uses humorous activism to advocate for social justice and ecology movements, sometimes as mock simulations for audiences to experience and reconsider their stances (Branagan, 2007). Feminist artists in Sweden have used music, theater, dance, and visual arts events and exhibitions to point out false and misleading representations of females; their objective is to reveal the truth about women's conditions, connect with social movements and create a counter hegemony (Rosenberg, 2009). Around the world, but especially in Europe, street art has emerged as a public way to express social messages that counter political platitudes and false information (Bacharach, 2015).

The National Arts Policy Roundtable (2008) reported on 21st century arts and civic engagement, asserting that arts-based civic engagement is vital for community improvement because it expresses new ways to view the world and offers a creative space to address social problems. Art increases social capital as it incentivizes cultural events and centers where people can connect and build trust, such as mural art programs and civic theater. Art expands civic participation by giving voice to those who might not normally participate in public discourse, and it can bring together people with divergent opinions to work together to envision new opportunities and solutions. For instance, when marginalized people were threatened with displacement, artists collaborated with the affected group to create joint art to show the possible impact on the community, which led to public dialogue about the project. Civic engagement also benefits the arts because it satisfies the public's heightened expectations for engaging in art experiences, and it enables the arts to work for the public good. To optimize arts civic engagement, the Roundtable recommended policies, practices and opportunities that advance and publicize the arts' role in improving the community and fostering citizen participation, and they encouraged strategic alliances across sectors to establish common goals between the arts and civic entities. The Roundtable's umbrella organization, Americans for the Arts, has sponsored several civic engagement art programs: Animating Democracy, advocacy efforts, research, networks, workshops and forums with local arts agencies to improve social efficacy of artists engaging civically.

Focusing on youth civic engagement through the arts, Rogers et al. (2015) asserted that arts and creative media help youth express their self-identity and engage meaningfully with the social and cultural public. Particularly as young people can leverage multimodal intertextuality, they can draw upon popular culture to remix cultural artifacts in an effort to critique that culture and speak to social transformation of interest to youth. Youth who have been under-represented or marginalized can artistically voice how they perceive and experience oppression and provide counter narratives that can contribute to networked publics. Through their artistic civic engagement, youth can critically understand their own positions relative to social and power networks, and analyze those networks to gain agency. Rogers and his colleagues mentioned several compelling youth-based artistic projects, which could be applied to issues of fake news: creating zines, talking to the community through film about violence, performing and staging bodies in motion to express social issues.

References

American Psychological Association. (2020). *Civic engagement*. Washington, DC: American Psychological Association.

Armfield, S., & Blocher, M. (2019). Global digital citizenship: Providing context. *TechTrends, 63*(4), 470–476.

Bacharach, S. (2015). Street art and consent. *The British Journal of Aesthetics, 55*(4), 481–495.

Barrett, M. (2018). Young people's civic and political engagement and global citizenship. *UN Chronicle, 54*(4). https://unchronicle.un.org/article/young-people-s-civic-and-political-engagement-and-global-citizenship

Bennett, W. (2008). Changing citizenship in the digital age. In W. Bennett (Ed.), *Civic life online: Learning how digital media can engage youth* (pp. 1–24). Cambridge, MA: The MIT Press.

Bennett, W., Wells, C., & Rank, A. (2009). Young citizens and civic learning: Two paradigms of citizenship in the digital age. *Citizenship Studies, 13*(2), 105–120.

Bhimji, F. (2016). Collaborations and performative agency in refugee theater in Germany. *Journal of Immigrant & Refugee Studies, 14*(1), 83–103.

Bobek, D., Zaff, J., Li, Y., & Lerner, R. M. (2009). Cognitive, emotional, and behavioral components of civic action: Towards an integrated measure of civic engagement. *Journal of Applied Developmental Psychology, 30*, 615–627.

Bohman, J. (2004). Expanding dialogue: The Internet, the public sphere and prospects for transnational democracy. *The Sociological Review, 52*, 131–155.

Branagan, M. (2007). The last laugh: Humour in community activism. *Community Development Journal, 42*(4), 470–481.

Branson, M. (1998). *The role of civic education.* Washington, DC: The Center for Civic Education.

Cho, A., Byrne, B., & Aelter, Z. (2020). *Digital civic engagement by young people.* New York, NY: UNICEF.

Choi, M. (2016). A concept analysis of digital citizenship for democratic citizenship education in the internet age. *Theory & Research in Social Education, 44*(4), 565–607.

Cohen, C., Kahne, J., Bowyer, B., Middaugh, E., & Rogowski, J. (2012). *Participatory politics: new media and youth political action.* Oakland, CA: MacArthur Research Network on Youth and Participatory Politics.

Community Partners. (2020). *Tapping journalism's civic power.* Los Angeles, CA: Community Powers.

Council of Europe. (2016). *Reference framework of competences for democratic culture.* Strasbourg, France: Council of Europe.

Dahlgren, P. (2005). The Internet, public spheres, and political communication: Dispersion and deliberation. *Political Communication, 22*(2), 147–162.

D'Costa, K. (2016, November 28). Understanding the social capital of fake news. *Scientific American.* https://blogs.scientificamerican.com/anthropology-in-practice/understanding-the-social-capital-of-fake-news/

Diez-Gutierrez, E., & Diaz-Nafria, J. (2018). Ubiquitous learning ecologies for a critical cybercitizenship. *Comunicar, 54*, 49–58.

European Citizen Science Association. (2015). *Ten principles of citizen science.* Berlin, Germany: European Citizen Science Association.

Fleming, J. (2017). News literacy and a civics model for journalism education. Paper presented at the First Global News Literacy Conference, August 14, Stony Brook, NY. https://commons.library.stonybrook.edu/cnlglobalconference/cnl2017/one/2/

Floridi, L. (2010). *Information: A very short introduction.* Oxford, UK: Oxford University Press.

Frau-Meigs, D., O'Neill, B., Soriani, A., & Tome, V. (2017). *Digital citizenship education: Overview and new perspectives.* Strasbourg, France: Council of Europe Publishing.

Freelon, D., Wells, C., & Bennett, L. (2013). Participation in the youth civic web: Assessing user activity levels in web sites presenting two civic styles. *Journal of Information Technology & Politics, 10*(3), 293–309.

G7 Science Academies. (2019). Citizen science in the Internet era. Summit of the G7 science academies, March 25–26, Ottawa, ON. https://rsc-src.ca/sites/default/files/Citizen%20G7%202019.pdf

Garlough, C. (2008). On the political uses of folklore: Performance and grassroots feminist activism in India. *Journal of American Folklore*, 167–191.

Generation Citizen. (2019). *360 civic learning: A study of the practices that cultivate civic engagement among youth from underserved communities.* New York, NY: Generation Citizen.

Gingold, J. (2013). *Building an evidence-based practice of action civics.* Medford, MA: Tufts University.

Giroux, H. (2005). *Schooling and the struggle for public life.* (2nd ed.). Boulder, CO: Paradigm.

Gleason, B., & Von Gillern, S. (2018). Digital citizenship with social media: Participatory practices of teaching and learning in secondary education. *Journal of Educational Technology & Society, 21*(1), 200–212.

Gould, J. (2011). *Guardian of democracy: The civic mission of schools.* Philadelphia, PA: Leonore Annenberg Institute for Civics.

Grijalva-Verdugo, A., & Moreno-Candil, D. (2017). Social empowerment in Mexican violent context through media competence. *Comunicar, 53*(25), 29–37.

Guilfoile, L., & Delander, B. (2014). *Guidebook: Six proven practices for effective civic learning.* Denver, CO: Education Commission of the States.

Haigh, M., Haigh, T., & Kozak, N. I. (2018). Stopping fake news: The work practices of peer-to-peer counter propaganda. *Journalism Studies, 19*(14), 2062–2087.

Hollandsworth, R., Donovan, J., & Welch, M. (2017). Digital citizenship: You can't go home again. *TechTrends, 61*(6), 524–530.

Hunter, P. (2016). The communications gap between scientists and public. *EMBO Reports, 17*(11), 1513–1515.

International Society for Technology in Education. (2016). *ISTE standards for students.* Eugene, OR: International Society for Technology in Education.

Jenkins, H. (2009). *Confronting the challenges of participatory culture: Media education for the 21st century.* Cambridge, MA: MIT Press.

Kahne, J., Hodgin, E., & Eidman-Aadahl, E. (2016). Redesigning civic education for the digital age: Participatory politics and the pursuit of democratic engagement. *Theory & Research in Social Education, 44*(1), 1–35.

Kligler-Vilenchik, N., & Shresthova, S. (2012). *Click activism: Youth civic engagement through online participatory cultures.* Los Angeles, CA: University of Southern California.

Krahanbuhl, K. (2017). A classical approach to educating for a civil society. *ASCD Express, 13*(6). www.ascd.org/ascd-express/vol13/1306-zemelman.aspx

Lema-Blanco, I., Rodriguez-Gomez, E.-F., & Barranquero-Carretero, A. (2016). Youth and the third sector media in Spain: Communication and social change training. *Comunicar, 48*(24), 91–99.

Levy, B. L., Solomon, B. G., & Collet-Gildard, L. (2016). Fostering political interest among youth during the 2012 presidential election: Instructional opportunities and challenges in a swing state. *Educational Researcher, 45*(9), 483–495.

Lievrouw, L., & Farb, S. (2003). Information and equity. *Annual Review of Information Science and Technology, 37*(1), 499–540.

Lindsay, J., & Davis, V. (2012). *Flattening classrooms, engaging minds: Move to global collaboration one step at a time.* Boston, MA: Pearson/Allyn and Bacon.

McGarry, A., Erhart, I., Eslen-Ziya, H, Jenzen, O., & Korkut, U. (Eds.). (2020). *The aesthetics of global protest: Visual culture and communication.* Amsterdam, Netherlands: Amsterdam University Press.

McGrew, S., Ortega, T., Breakstone, J., & Wineburg, S. (2017). The challenge that's bigger than fake news: Civic reasoning in a social media environment. *American Educator, 41*(3), 4–10.

Middaugh, E., Clark, L., & Ballard, P. (2017). Digital media, participatory politics and positive youth development. *Pediatrics, 140*(Supplement 2), S127–S131.

Middaugh, E., & Kirshner, B. (2015). *#youthaction: Becoming political in the digital age.* Charlotte, NC: Information Age Publishing.

Mukerjee, M. (2017, July 14). How fake news goes viral—here's the math. *Scientific American.* www.scientificamerican.com/article/how-fake-news-goes-viral-mdash-heres-the-math/.

National Arts Policy Roundtable. (2008). *The arts and civic engagement: Strengthening the 21st century community.* Washington, DC: Americans for the Arts.

OECD. (2018). *Youth engagement and empowerment in Jordan, Morocco and Tunisia.* Paris, France: OECD.

OECD. (2017). Citizens with a say. Trends shaping education spotlight 13. www.oecd.org/education/ceri/Spotlight-13-Citizens-with-a-say.pdf

OECD. (2003). *Promise and problems of e-democracy: Challenges of online citizen engagement.* Paris, France: OECD.

Orth, D., & Chen, E. (2013). The strategy for digital citizenship. *Independent School, 72*(4), 56–63.

Parekh, B. (2003). Cosmopolitanism and global citizenship. *Review of International Studies, 29*(1), 3–17.

Parker, L. (2020). Fighting for their future. *National Geographic, 237*(4), 70–83.

Pennell, S., & Fede, B. (2018). Fighting fake news: Interdisciplinary online literacies for social justice. *Voices from the Middle, 25*(4), 48–53.

Pentney, B. A. (2008). Feminism, activism, and knitting: Are the fibre arts a viable mode for feminist political action? *Thirdspace, 8*(1). http://journals.sfu.ca/thirdspace/index.php/journal/article/view/%20pentney/210

Peters, A., Tartari, E., Lotfinejad, N., Parneix, P., & Pittet, D. (2018). Fighting the good fight: The fallout of fake news in infection prevention and why context matters. *Journal of Hospital Infection, 100*(4), 365–370.

Peters, M. A., & Besley, T. (2019). Citizen science and post-normal science in a post-truth era: Democratising knowledge; socialising responsibility. *Educational Philosophy and Theory, 51*(13), 1293–1303.

Pinazo-Calatayud, D., Nos-Aldas, E., & Agut-Nieto, S. (2020). Positive or negative communication in social activism. *Comunicar, 62*, 69–78.

Pinto, B., Costa, J., & Cabral, H. (2017). How do science communication practitioners view scientists and audiences in relation to public engagement activities? A research note concerning the marine sciences in Portugal. *Bulletin of Science, Technology & Society, 37*(3), 159–166.

Pogue, D. (2017). The ultimate cure for the fake news epidemic will be more skeptical readers. *Scientific American, 316*(2), 24.

Rabkin, N. (2017). *Hearts and minds: The arts and civic engagement.* San Francisco, CA: James Irvin Foundation.

Rasmussen, L. M. (2019). Confronting research misconduct in citizen science. *Citizen Science: Theory and Practice, 4*(1). https://theoryandpractice.citizenscienceassociation.org/article/10.5334/cstp.207/

Ribble, M. (2015). *Digital citizenship in schools.* Eugene, OR: International Society for Technology in Education.

Rogers, T., Winters, K-L., Perry, M., & LaMonde, A-M. (2015). *Youth, critical literacies, and civic engagement: Arts, media, and literacy in the lives of adolescents.* New York, NY: Routledge.

Rosenberg, T. (2009). On feminist activist aesthetics. *Journal of Aesthetics & Culture, 1*(1), 1–12.

Rubin, V. L. (2019). Disinformation and misinformation triangle: A conceptual model for "fake news" epidemic, causal factors and interventions. *Journal of Documentation, 75*(5), 1013–1034.

Saura, G., Munoz-Moreno, J., Luengo-Navas, J., & Martos-Ortega, J. (2017). Protesting on Twitter: Citizenship and empowerment from public education. *Comunicar, 53*(25), 39–48.

Schulz, W., Ainley, J., Fraillon, J., Losito, B., & Agrusti, G. (2016). *IEA International Civic and Citizenship Education Study 2016 Assessment Framework.* Amsterdam, Netherlands: International Association for the Evaluation of Educational Achievement.

Senabre, E., Ferran-Ferrer, N., & Perello, J. (2018). Participatory design of citizen science experiments. *Comunicar, 54*, 29–38.

Siapera, E., & Veglis, A. (Eds.) (2012). *The handbook of global online journalism.* Malden, MA: Wiley-Blackwell.

Stern, M., & Seifert, S. (2009). *Civic engagement and the arts: Issues of conceptualization and measurement.* Philadelphia, PA: University of Pennsylvania.

Todd, M. (2018, October 10). Citizen social scientists edit day's news with new tool. *Social Science Space.* www.socialsciencespace.com/2018/10/citizen-social-scientists-edit-days-news-with-new-tool/

True/False 2020. (2020). Reality, fiction, foresight. *Center for Media & Social Impact.* https://cmsimpact.org/fair-use-blog/truefalse-2020-reality-fiction-foresight/

UNESCO. (2015). *Global citizenship education: Topics and learning objectives.* Paris, France: UNESCO.

UNESCO Bangkok. (2015). *Fostering digital citizenship through safe and responsible use of ICT.* Bangkok, Thailand: UNESCO.

United Nations Department of Economic and Social Affairs. (2016). *World youth report on youth civic engagement.* New York, NY: United Nations.

U.S. Department of Education. (2012). *Advancing civic learning and engagement in democracy: A road map and call to action.* Washington, DC: U.S. Department of Education.

Walters, M., Gee, D., & Mohammed, S. (2019). A literature review: Digital citizenship and the elementary educator. *International Journal of Technology in Education, 2*(1), 1–21.

Warren-Riley, S. & Hurley, E. (2017). Multimodal pedagogical approaches to public writing: Digital media advocacy and mundane texts. *Composition Forum, 36*(1). www.learntechlib.org/p/191960/.

Wells, C. (2015). *The civic organisation and the digital citizen.* Oxford, UK: Oxford University Press.

Westheimer, J., & Kahne, J. (2004). Educating the 'good' citizen: Political choices and pedagogical goals. *PS: Political Science and Politics, 37*(2), 241–247.

Youth.gov (2020). *Civic engagement.* Washington, DC: Youth.gov. https://youth.gov/youth-topics/civic-engagement-and-volunteering

7
THE CURRICULUM CONTEXT

Even though fake news impacts society daily, it is typically unevenly incorporated into educational curriculum, be it a stand-alone "one-shot" lesson, a separate unit, or integrated into existing courses. Such opportunities should not be missed, especially as fake news can serve as a "gateway" topic to motivate learners to hone underlying literacies needed to identify and respond to fake news: news literacy, media literacy, visual literacy, digital literacy, data literacy, as well as information literacy. Ideally, a fake-news infused curriculum should be an organization-wide initiative that meets the needs of its stakeholders. This chapter describes model fake news curricula, and provides representative existing curricula that address news literacy and fake news.

Curriculum issues

While the study of news media has not been integrated well into traditional curricula, its impact on political and daily decision-making contexts highlights its need to be part of both formal and informal education. Developing and implementing fake news curriculum can be daunting. As previously noted, fake news is typically couched within news literacy, which may be considered a subset of media literacy. Not only is fake news sometimes a problematic term, but even the definition of media and of literacy can be challenging. Therefore, the first step in developing such a curriculum is to develop a mutual understanding of the above terms and to operationalize them.

Competencies

The next step is to agree what it means to be able to discern, evaluate and address fake news. Typical competences are listed in Table 7.1, aligned with relevant literacies.

TABLE 7.1 Fake news competencies and literacies

Literacies>	News	Visual	Audio	Data	Digital	Media	Information
IDENTIFY FAKE NEWS							
Identify what is news	x					x	x
Identify what is fake news	x					x	x
Check the news currency	x					x	x
Examine the entire news story	x	x	x	x	x	x	x
Determine the news purpose	x					x	x
Determine the target audience	x					x	x
Trace the source of news	x				x	x	x
Assess the creator's authority	x						x
Determine point of view	x					x	x
Distinguish fact from opinion	x						x
Determine the tone and vocabulary	x	x	x			x	
Examine connotative or emotional aspects	x	x	x	x	x	x	x
Identify values or beliefs	x	x					x
Identify cultural connotations	x	x	x			x	x
Determine what is omitted	x	x		x		x	x
Determine the impact of format	x	x	x	x	x	x	
Analyze use of visuals	x	x				x	x
Analyze use of sound	x		x			x	
Analyze use of data	x	x		x	x		
Assess labels and captions	x	x		x			x
Determine visual manipulation	x	x				x	
Determine sound manipulation	x		x			x	
Determine data manipulation	x	x		x	x		

TABLE 7.1 Cont.

Literacies>	News	Visual	Audio	Data	Digital	Media	Information
Determine if it is satire or parody	x	x	x			x	x
Verify supporting evidence	x	x		x			x
Assess research methods						x	
Verify with content experts	x	x		x			x
Determine if bots are used					x		
Use a fact-checker	x	x		x	x		
Check number of hits or likes						x	
Compare news coverage consistency in same source	x	x	x	x	x	x	x
Assess transparency of source process	x	x	x	x	x	x	x
Check source's mission, sponsor, finances							
Assess source's ads							
Compare news coverage of other sources	x	x	x	x	x	x	x
Identify reputable sources							
Determine how specialized information impacts news							
ADDRESSING FAKE NEWS							
Explain the impact of real and fake news	x	x	x	x	x	x	x
Explain how news is produced and disseminated	x				x	x	x
Analyze the history of fake news	x				x	x	x
Explain why people believe fake news	x				x		x
Determine what news to pay attention to	x	x	x	x	x	x	x
Determine what news to select to consume	x	x	x	x	x	x	x

(continued)

TABLE 7.1 Cont.

Literacies>	*News*	*Visual*	*Audio*	*Data*	*Digital*	*Media*	*Information*
Consider personal biases	x	x	x	x	x	x	x
Know when to look for more news	x	x	x	x	x	x	x
Determine when to respond to news	x				x	x	x
Determine how to respond to news	x	x	x	x	x	x	x
Determine what news to share	x				x	x	x
Determine how to share news					x	x	x
Know how to communicate news	x	x	x	x	x	x	x
Know how to communicate counter news	x	x	x	x	x	x	x
Know whom to contact about fake news	x				x	x	x
Engage civically to address fake news	x	x	x	x	x	x	x
PERSONAL RESPONSIBILITY							
Know how to set privacy and security settings					x	x	
Practice appropriate, responsible interactions							x
Maintain an open mindset							x
Accept and seek other points of view							x
Keep learning							x
Comply with copyright law						x	x
Self-regulate news behavior						x	x
Manage your digital footprint						x	

This table explicitly links fake news competencies to relevant literacies, which can help educational organizations align fake news content and skills to existing student learning outcomes. In the same way, the chapter on the various literacies supporting fake news competences lists literacy standards that can be used to design a curriculum.

Developing a curriculum

Summarizing, then, core elements of fake news curriculum typically include:

- Definition and variations of fake news.
- Need for news media literacy.
- The communication cycle of fake news.
- Identification and discernment of fake news.
- Credible sources and organizations, including libraries.
- Dealing with fake news.

Strong additional options may include the history of fake news, medium-specific characteristics, and civic engagement.

News literacy curriculum is most typically found in journalism and communication studies programs. Otherwise, news literacy is seldom explicitly developed, let alone fake news. In Europe, news literacy tends to be integrated in various subject matter, while in the United States, news literacy is usually treated as a separate stand-alone subject (Potter, 2010). Nevertheless, it should be obvious that no one curriculum fits everyone – or is perfect. Rather, formal and informal organizations should determine the overall curriculum and desired learning outcomes that aligns with their mission and existing standards, and best serves their community and situation (Potter, 2010).

At the least, decision-makers should determine the depth of knowledge and breadth of skills that learners should demonstrate. Again, existing standards often provide indicators that describe the quality and extent of competence. The chapter on fake news literacies mentions several applicable standards. These competency decisions should consider the targeted learner population, teaching expertise, available material and fiscal resources, available time, the existing curriculum, and the mission of the institution or organization. For instance, primary children might focus on fact versus fiction or credibility using television advertisements as the context while senior citizens might address the same concept in terms of Internet scams. A secondary school language arts course might incorporate fake news in terms of narration, different writing genres, and rhetoric. Fake news could serve as a fulcrum for research skills or career exploration.

The next step involves determining who will teach this curriculum, ranging from a one-shot lesson taught by a librarian or a journalist to a full course. The approach could range from a stand-alone public service announcement to a school-wide integrated structure. While any exposure is better than none, situating fake news instruction into subject areas is usually more meaningful and lends itself better to practice and relevant application (Huguet et al., 2019). Whatever the decision, all learners should experience the curriculum.

A school-wide effort, particularly in K-12 settings, offers the greatest potential as it signals the responsibility of all of the stakeholders, from principal to staff and families. It thus negates the message that fake news is a journalism or a library "thing." Ideally, all the teaching faculty should agree on the learning outcomes. Then they can examine their current curriculum to see if those concepts and skills are already addressed, such as critical thinking, point of view, writing tone, oral presentation skills, citation practices and research skills. This coordinating exercise also enables faculty to learn what each other is teaching, which can reduce duplicative instruction and, instead, help learners progress faster and deeper as well as foster school-wide collaboration and cross-disciplinary knowledge. By identifying existing curriculum, faculty can then easily identify remaining gaps for fake news related curriculum, and decide which course will address the issue. For instance, language arts teachers might have students learn how news is produced, mathematics classes might study how to lie with statistics, science teachers can have students investigate pseudo-science, and history classes can explore and analyze the impact of fake news primary sources. Co-curriculum should also be considered in terms of service clubs; furthermore, the school council might add a service learning graduation requirement. While the idea of a compulsory media literacy or news literacy subject remains controversial (Debating Europe, 2020), regardless of the curriculum or approach, all students should have opportunities to learn and practice news media literacy, including fake news.

Instructional design and strategies

Once the venue and content are set, the teachers can design the instruction. How will learners be assessed? What content will be covered? What resources will be used so learners can gain knowledge? What activities will learners engage in to practice skills? In many cases, technology should be integrated since so much news is communicated via media. What constraints exist, such as time or space?

In terms of resources, teachers might have to decide whether to use existing curricular units in their entirety, curate existing instructional materials, create original resources, or incorporate a mixture of sources to meet the particular needs of their learners. Whenever possible, teachers should provide learners with choices of resources, ways to engage, and ways to act.

Most news and media experts agree that instruction should start with gaining skills in consuming news critically but also provide opportunities for producing effective media messages (Jacobson, 2017). For instance, learners can use and develop criteria for identifying and evaluating news, then choose a fake news story to explore in more depth by comparing news treatments and researching the underlying issue; they can then create a media product to communicate their findings and make recommendations (Friesem, 2019). This kind of learning by doing also facilitates student engagement and makes the content more relevant. Similarly, fake news topics should build on learners' interests so that the subject matter will be relevant to them, such as fake news about celebrities, entertainment, health issues, food, disasters, and technology.

Open dialogue constitutes another important instructional strategy. Learners should have opportunities to experience a variety of news from a variety of perspectives, and engage in meaningful reflection and discussion about those differences in class. Teachers bring subject expertise to help learners evaluate and interpret news, and can guide learners in navigating the complex and sometimes overwhelming media landscape. This practice is particularly effective when breaking news links with the academic subject matter, such as misleading statistics in math class or falsehoods about climate change in science (Head et al., 2019). Schools should also bridge academic knowledge with daily practices such as using social media; for instance, teachers can discuss with students about the consequences of sharing fake news – and the power of social media to mobilize positive social change.

Such acknowledgment of social networks also helps teachers bridge conceptual knowledge with community application; for instance, younger learners can observe how fake news affects their neighborhood (such as disease disinformation) and older learners can conduct action research to counter immigration disinformation. In reviewing civic education and youth development literacy efforts the National Action Civics Collaborative identified key learning outcomes of action research: civic and cultural transformation, informed and engaged citizenship, civic creation and positive youth leadership (Gingold, 2013). To achieve these outcomes, learners need the following competencies: civic knowledge, civic values, critical thinking, communication, collaboration, agency, professionalism and general academic skills. Four principles guide curriculum (Gingold, 2013, p. 6):

- Action, especially collective action.
- Youth voice, including experiences, knowledge, concerns and opinions.
- Youth agency, including action, authority and leadership.
- Reflection, especially as it enriches the process.

Instruction is only as effective as the extent of student learning. Assessing learners' fake news literacy can be challenging because such competency involves a complex set of knowledge, skills, dispositions and behaviors (Huguet et al., 2019). Furthermore, those competencies also depend on the context in which they are performed. At the least, teachers should measure both learner processes and products, ideally using rubrics with several essential criteria. Assessment should align with the institution's expectations, be practical and manageable, and empirically sound in terms of validity, reliability and fairness. Self-reporting tends to capture personal perception more than ability, and multiple-choice questions typically do not measure higher order learning. Authentic tasks and products are sometimes hard to assess but they represent more meaningful competence. Portfolios also offer a manageable method to build evidence of learning and application over time, especially if learners have to choose significant sample work and reflect on the way that it demonstrates learning.

Librarians' roles and collaboration

Because librarians evaluate and work with all kinds of information in various formats, they have unique knowledge and skills to help students – and teachers – learn about fake news and how to address it. Therefore, librarians should seek out opportunities across their community to provide news literacy tools to empower people. For instance, librarians frequently create library guides to help their constituents address fake news. As a welcoming and neutral affinity space for both the consumption and production of media, the library itself serves as a prime informal educational haven for news literacy and related literacies. Librarians can also play an active instructional role: teaching fake news-related literacy independently or in collaboration with their educational community and other stakeholders. Besides helping learners be informed news consumers, librarians and other educators can help learners be producers of information by curating news and serving as citizen journalists.

Each kind of library offers unique ways to address fake news. School librarians tend to focus on media and information literacy, and they collaborate with classroom teachers to guide engaging learning activities such as inquiry-based research to access and evaluate fake news sources as well as producing media messages to counter fake news (Agosto, 2018). Academic librarians tend to focus on supporting a range of research skills from a discipline approach, which helps students get the back story of fake news. Public librarians serve the entire community so they provide a range of programs that can address fake news: story hours that distinguish between fantasy and reality, teen media production workshops, group discussions about news-related movies, and panel discussions on fake news (American Library Association, 2018). Special librarians support agencies and industries with research about current news and trends behind fake news. All librarians gather, evaluate, organize and provide physical and intellectual access to news, and provide information services that guide people about fake news; they also incorporate technology to optimize their functions. As part of their civic engagement, librarians advocate for responsible news and fake news reform as well.

Sample news literacy and fake news curriculum

Here are general curricula about fake news and associated literacies.

- American Library Association Programming Librarian: www.programming librarian.org/sites/default/files/media_literacy_your_library_-_final_report_ dec_2018.pdf
- Caulfield, M. (2020). *Web literacy for student fact-checkers:* https://webliteracy. pressbooks.com/

- Center for Media Literacy: www.medialit.org/educator-resources
- Center for News Literacy: http://drc.centerfornewsliteracy.org/course-pack
- Common Sense Media: www.commonsense.org/education/toolkit/
- Coursera news literacy: www.coursera.org/learn/news-literacy
- Dutch media literacy: www.mediawijzer.net/
- First Draft News: https://firstdraftnews.org/free-online-course-on-identi fying-misinformation/
- National Association for Media Literacy Education: https://namle.net/2014/ 11/01/teaching-democracy-a-media-literacy-approach/
- The News Literary Project: www.thenewsliteracyproject.org/
- Newseum education: https://newseumed.org/unit/believe-it-or-not/ and https://newseumed.org/stack/media-literacy-resources/
- Project Look Sharp: www.projectlooksharp.org/?action=news-accuracy
- Stony Book University Digital Resource Center: https://digitalresource. center/
- Swedish media literacy: https://mikoteket.se/
- Teaching Tolerance digital literacy: www.tolerance.org/frameworks/digital-literacy
- UNESCO journalism education: https://en.unesco.org/fightfakenews
- UNESCO handbook for journalism education and training: https://en.unesco. org/sites/default/files/journalism_fake_news_disinformation_print_friendly_ 0.pdf

One-shot presentation example

1. What is fake news?
   - Fake news is deliberate, published disinformation/hoax/lie purported to be real news.
   - Distinguish between different types of misleading information: http:// pbs.twimg.com/media/DEnxvISXoAAyRg8.png
2. What's the big deal about fake news?
   - During the latter part of the 2016 Presidential campaign, fake news was shared and commented more than real news, according to the following Buzzfeed report: www.buzzfeednews.com/article/craigsilverman/viral-fake-election-news-outperformed-real-news-on-facebook.
   - 75 percent of us fall for fake headlines, according to this 2016 Ipsos Poll: www.buzzfeednews.com/article/craigsilverman/fake-news-survey.
   - Almost a quarter of adults have shared a made-up news story, according to this Pew Research Center study: www.journalism.org/2016/12/ 15/many-americans-believe-fake-news-is-sowing-confusion/?utm_ source=Pew+Research+Center&utm_campaign=e080af4f66-EMAIL_ CAMPAIGN_2016_12_14&utm_medium=email&utm_term=0_ 3e953b9b70-e080af4f66-400229353.

- The study also found that two-thirds of adults say that fake news leads them to be confused about basic facts of current news, although more than three-quarters feel at least somewhat confident about being able to recognize fake news.
- A 2016 research study by Stanford faculty (https://purl.stanford.edu/fv751yt5934) focused on students' news literacy tasks, and found that middle and high school students, and even some in college, have trouble distinguishing which online resources are credible.

3. What are the consequences of fake news?
   - When people believe fake news, they are misinformed, and may make poor decisions. When people don't know what to believe, they may become frustrated, polarized, confused, fearful, distrustful, cynical and withdrawn. None of this helps society.
   - Watch C-SPAN's video on fake news sites and effects on democracy: www.c-span.org/classroom/document/?6004

4. How does fake news become news?
   - Watch *Teaching Tolerance's* video to see how fake news becomes news: https://youtu.be/qcRWkkSvfj0

5. What looks like fake news?
   - Which one is #FakeNews?: https://choices.scholastic.com/issues/2016–17/050117/which-one-is – fakenews.html

6. Why do we believe fake news?
   - It's compelling: novel, strong words and images, good storytelling, like gossip.
   - It's believable.
   - It confirms our beliefs.
   - Faced with facts, people with lower cognitive ability have a harder time changing their attitudes.
   - Watch this video on Media and the Mind: www.youtube.com/watch?v=TAdkzxB4WFo

7. How do you choose your news?
   - Get good advice on choosing valid news from this TED Ed video "How do you choose your news?": www.youtube.com/watch?v=q-Y-z6HmRgI&feature=youtu.be
   - Evaluate media outlets: www.allgeneralizationsarefalse.com/wp-content/uploads/2018/01/Media-Bias-Chart_Version-3.1_Watermark-min.jpg
   - Use your local libraries – and work with their librarians.

8. Be a fact-checker
   - Use this IFLA infographic to spot fake news: www.ifla.org/publications/node/11174
   - Four ways to fact-check:
     - Look through (read through the entire website and links): California State University, Chico Evaluating information – Applying the CRAAP test: https://library.csuchico.edu/help/source-or-information-good

- Look up (trace the source): How journalists verify stories from social media: www.journalism.co.uk/news-features/how-to-verify-content-from-social-media/s5/a548645/
- Look across (other sources): AllSides (www.allsides.com/unbiased-balanced-news) rates media bias, and searches across the political spectrum to provide balanced news.
- Look inside (what are your own beliefs and biases?)

9. Try your ability to identify fake news
   - Factitious: http://factitious.augamestudio.com/#/
10. Now you won't be faked out by the news!

WebQuest on fake news (long version)

Topic I: Identifying Fake News

A. Introduction

As recent politics have made abundantly clear, news (i.e., a report of current events) might not be as true as it appears. At the same time, mass media play an increasingly significant role in today's society. More than ever, we need to consciously and critically analyze and evaluate mass media messages, such as the news, and then decide how to respond. This WebQuest provides resources that can help you and your community be savvy media consumers and producers – and be an informed and contributing citizen. To this end, it focuses on fake news: deliberate, publicly published disinformation/hoax/lie purported to be real news. Don't get faked out by the news.

B. Task

Your task is to identify fake news. To help you in this task, you will work in groups of four, each person assuming a persona. Together, you will use your unique perspective to gain a deeper understanding of fake news and its context.

C. Resources: http://tinyurl.com/FakeNewsLibGuide

D. Processes

- *Prepare*:

  Arrange yourself in a group of four people. Choose one of these four personas: fake news creator, media outlet editor, politician, student; do not duplicate personas. Create a Google Doc (or equivalent) to document and share your work; all group members label their individual work by initializing it.

- *Background information:*

  Each person/persona investigates one background aspect of fake news, drawing upon the Fake News LibGuide: http://tinyurl.com/FakeNewsLibGuide. In the group Google Doc (or equivalent) under the heading "Background" (citing the source of information), each person posts four relevant facts that impact identifying fake news, drawn from at least two sources.

- Media outlet publisher (e.g., newspaper or TV): communication cycle (under Background).
- Fake news creator: Advertising techniques (under Literacies: Media Literacy).
- Teen or college student: Processing fake news (under Discerning Fake News).
- Politician: Consequences of fake news (under Home).

- *Strategies:*
  As a group, read about strategies to uncover fake news (under Discerning Fake News). Divide the resources such that each person is responsible for three documents (one general website, one authored article, and one video). In the group Google Doc (or equivalent) under the heading "Strategies" (citing the source of information), each person posts six relevant facts (two from each source) that impact identifying fake news.

- *Literacies:*
  Literacy is a basic requirement for discerning fake news. As a group, read about literacies that support the ability to identify fake news. Each person/ persona investigates one literacy that informs identifying fake news, drawing upon the Fake News Literacies section of the LibGuide: http:// tinyurl.com/FakeNewsLibGuide. In the group Google Doc (or equivalent) under the heading "Literacies" (citing the source of information), each person posts four relevant facts that impact identifying fake news, drawn from at least two sources.
  - Media outlet editor: Media Literacy.
  - Fake news creator: News Literacy.
  - Student: Information Literacy.
  - Politician: Visual Literacy.

- *Fact-checking:*
  1. As a warm-up exercise, your group goes to Factitious (http://facti-tious.augamestudio.com/#/) and plays the game that tests news sense (start with "quick start"). As each news item appears, decide individually whether the item is real or fake, drawing upon your unique background and strategy notes. Then as a group, come to consensus, justifying the stance by sharing the individual notes.
  2. As a group, go to the document "Fake, misleading, clickbait-y, and satirical 'news' sources" (http://d279m997dpfwgl.cloudfront.net/ wp/2016/11/Resource-False-Misleading-Clickbait-y-and-Satirical-%E2%80%9CNews%E2%80%9D-Sources-1.pdf). Choose two news sources from category 1, and then as a group choose one news story from each of the two news sources.
  3. As a group, go to the fact-checking tools (under Discerning Fake News). Divide the resources such that each person is responsible for two fact-checking tools.

4. Now it is time for the group to be fact-checkers. For each news story, each person checks its authenticity using the two fact-checking tools. Each person compares the results for each news story, and posts the comparison on the group Google Doc (or equivalent) under the heading "Fact-Checking," separating the two news stories.

5. As a group, discuss your findings, and post your comments and suggested fact-checking strategies under the heading "Strategies" in the Google Doc (or equivalent).

6. Each person finds two news items/stories about a current event (e.g., government bill/executive order/court case, crisis, social issue (e.g., global change, human rights, immigration, terrorism)). One news item should be true and the other should be false. Strip the format (and omit any images) of the two news items/stories, and post them on the group Google Doc (or equivalent) under the heading "Fake or Real." There are a couple of ways to strip the format: paste the news items/stories into a word processing application (or even WordPad/ NotePad), or use a stripping tool such as www.striphtml.com/.

7. Each person chooses from the other person's two parallel news items/stories, and decides which one is true and which one is false, explaining how the authenticity was determined, and the possible impact of the fake news. Post the decision and explanation underneath the news items/stories.

8. Each person checks their peers' posting from step 7, and confirms or corrects the decision. If the decision differs, post the explanation for the original decision.
   - Each person writes a reflection, answering the following questions:
   - What did you learn about fake news?
   - What did you learn about identifying fake news?
   - How does this information about fake news apply to your own life?
   - Post the reflections in the group Google Doc (or equivalent) under the heading "Reflection."

E. Evaluation

The group Google Doc is evaluated according to these criteria:
- How well did each person in the group follow the directions?
- How relevant, accurate, thorough and well written was each entry?
- How complete and accurate was each citation?
- To what extent was the identification of each news item/story accurate and well-justified?

F. Conclusion

Now you know how to identify fake news. This is a critical skill, as you have found out, because it informs your decisions and consequential actions. It helps you be a capable citizen, and ultimately impacts the society in which you live. Good for you, Expert Fact-Checker!

Topic II: Addressing Fake News

A. Introduction
Fake news has real consequences in society, so it is imperative that each person learns how to identify fake news. Especially as fake news itself is likely to exist no matter what precautions are taken, it is ultimately each person's responsibility to be discerning news and media consumers. This WebQuest provides resources that can help you use the topic of fake news to inform your community to be savvy media consumers and producers – and be an informed and contributing citizen.

B. Task
Your task is to address fake news. To help you in this task, you will work in groups of four, each person assuming a persona. Together, you will use your unique perspective to develop a product that will educate others about fake news.

C. Resources: http://tinyurl.com/FakeNewsLibGuide

D. Processes
   1. Continue with the same group and personas. Use the same group Google Doc (or equivalent) to record and share information. There are several ways to address fake news. Each person/persona gathers facts about one aspect of addressing fake news. On the group Google Doc (or equivalent) under the heading "Addressing Fake News," each person posts four ideas (drawing upon, and citing, at least two sources).
      • Media outlet editor: Library's Role.
      • Fake news creator: Fixing Fake News (under Discerning Fake News).
      • Student: Digital Citizenship (under Civic Engagement).
      • Politician: Civics Instruction.
   2. Fake News curriculum can be integrated into formal and informal education in several ways, and the curriculum itself can vary according to the subject matter perspective, age, timeframe, delivery method, and so on. Each person/persona explores and compares two general curricula about fake news (under Curriculum: General Curriculum); be sure not to overlap websites. On the group Google Doc (or equivalent) under the heading "Curriculum," each person posts their comparison (and citation) of two curricula.
   3. The group as a whole chooses one curriculum to draw upon or modify (which can also be informed by the WebQuest activities done). They identify four concepts or skills about fake news that they want to convey.
   4. Podcasts/audio files are great for telling a story, doing public service announcements, and giving targeted facts. The group creates a four-part podcast media message series that addresses fake news, one idea per podcast,

based on their curriculum. Each podcast should take 30–60 seconds. Post the podcast and accompanying transcript on the group Google Doc (or equivalent) under the heading "Podcast."

TECHNICAL NOTE: You can make podcasts using GarageBand (on Macs), Windows Voice Recorder and Windows Sound Recorder (although the latter do not have editing features). A good free tool is Audacity (http://audacity.sourceforge.net), which then needs to be encoded (typically with LAME: http://lame.sourceforge.net/) into an MPG3 file in order to be broadcast. A good tutorial with downloads is www.how-to-podcast-tutorial.com/13-basic-podcasting-software.htm.   http://elearningindustry.com/free-podcast-tools is another good collection of podcasting tools and resources.

5. Each person writes a reflection, answering the following questions:
    *   What did you learn about addressing fake news?
    *   What did you learn about informing others about fake news?
    *   How does this information about fake news apply to your own life?
6. Post the reflections in the Google Doc (or equivalent) under the heading "Podcast Reflection."

E. Evaluation
    1. The group Google Doc is evaluated according to these criteria:
        *   How well did each person in the group follow the directions?
        *   How relevant, accurate, thorough and well written was each entry?
        *   How complete and accurate was each citation?
    2. The group's podcasts are evaluated according to these criteria:
        *   Content: Creative and original content; catchy and clever introduction; relevant and accurate information; clear engaging purpose; clear summary of key information; appropriately credited quotes and sources of information.
        *   Delivery: Well-rehearsed, smooth delivery in a conversational style; highly effective enunciation, expression and rhythm keep the audience listening; correct grammar throughout the podcast.
        *   Technical production: Smooth and appropriate transitions with noisy or dead spaces; appropriate volume of voice, music and effects; length of 1–2 minutes.
        *   Complete, accurate and error-free transcript.

F. Conclusion
Now you know how to address fake news and inform others about fake news. You are modeling pro-active digital citizenship. Good for you – and your community!

WebQuest on fake news (shorter version)

Identifying Fake News

A. Introduction

As recent politics have made abundantly clear, news (i.e., a report of current events) might not be as true as it appears. At the same time, mass media play an increasingly significant role in today's society. More than ever, we need to consciously and critically analyze and evaluate mass media messages, such as the news, and then decide how to respond. This WebQuest provides resources that can help you and your community be savvy media consumers and producers – and be an informed and contributing citizen. To this end, it focuses on fake news: deliberate, publicly published disinformation/hoax/lie purported to be real news. Don't get faked out by the news.

B. Task

Your task is to identify fake news. To help you in this task, you will work in groups of four, each person assuming a persona. Together, you will use your unique perspective to gain a deeper understanding of fake news and its context.

C. Resources: http://tinyurl.com/FakeNewsLibGuide

D. Processes

- *Prepare*:

  Arrange yourself in a group of four people. Choose one of these four personas: fake news creator, media outlet editor, politician, student; do not duplicate personas. Create a Google Doc (or equivalent) to document and share your work; all group members label their individual work by initializing it.

- *Background information*:

  Each person/persona investigates one background aspect of fake news, drawing upon the Fake News LibGuide: http://tinyurl.com/FakeNewsLibGuide. In the group Google Doc (or equivalent) under the heading "Background" (citing the source of information), each person posts four relevant facts that impact identifying fake news, drawn from at least two sources.

  - Media outlet publisher (e.g., newspaper or TV): communication cycle (under Background).
  - Fake news creator: Advertising techniques (under Literacies: Media Literacy).
  - Teen or college student: Processing fake news (under Discerning Fake News).
  - Politician: Consequences of fake news (under Home).

- *Literacies*:

  Literacy is a basic requirement for discerning fake news. As a group, read about literacies that support the ability to identify fake news. Each person/persona investigates one literacy that informs identifying fake news, drawing upon the Fake News Literacies section of the LibGuide: http://tinyurl.com/FakeNewsLibGuide. In the group Google Doc (or equivalent) under the heading "Literacies" (citing the source of information), each person posts four relevant facts that impact identifying fake news, drawn from at least two sources.

- Media outlet editor: Media Literacy.
- Fake news creator: News Literacy.
- Student: Information Literacy.
- Politician: Visual Literacy.
- *Fact-checking:*
  1. As a warm-up exercise, your group goes to Factitious (http://factitious.augamestudio.com/#/) and plays the game that tests news sense (start with "quick start"). As each news item appears, decide individually whether the item is real or fake, drawing upon your unique background and strategy notes. Then as a group, come to consensus, justifying the stance by sharing the individual notes.
  2. As a group, go to the document "Fake, misleading, clickbait-y, and satirical 'news' sources" (http://d279m997dpfwgl.cloudfront.net/wp/2016/11/Resource-False-Misleading-Clickbait-y-and-Satirical-%E2%80%9CNews%E2%80%9D-Sources-1.pdf). Choose two news sources from category 1, and then as a group choose one news story from each of the two news sources.
  3. As a group, go to the fact-checking tools (under Discerning Fake News). Divide the resources such that each person is responsible for two fact-checking tools.
  4. Now it is time for the group to be fact-checkers. For each news story, each person checks its authenticity using the two fact-checking tools. Each person compares the results for each news story, and posts the comparison on the group Google Doc (or equivalent) under the heading "Fact-Checking," separating the two news stories.
  5. Each person checks their peers' posting from step 4, and confirms or corrects the decision. If the decision differs, post the explanation for the original decision.
     - Each person writes a reflection, answering the following questions:
     - What did you learn about fake news?
     - What did you learn about identifying fake news?
     - How does this information about fake news apply to your own life?
     - Post the reflections in the group Google Doc (or equivalent) under the heading "Reflection."

E. Evaluation

The group Google Doc is evaluated according to these criteria:

- How well did each person in the group follow the directions?
- How relevant, accurate, thorough and well written was each entry?
- How complete and accurate was each citation?

- To what extent was the identification of each news item/story accurate and well-justified?

F. Conclusion

Now you know how to identify fake news. This is a critical skill, as you have found out, because it informs your decisions and consequential actions. It helps you be a capable citizen, and ultimately impacts the society in which you live. Good for you, Expert Fact-Checker!

Fake news: A middle school curriculum

1. What is fake news?
   - Ask learners to share their perceptions of fake news. They can make a concept map about fake news. Share their perceptions.
   - Define fake news: "Fake news is deliberate, published disinformation/ hoax/lie purported to be real news."
   - Compare fake news with other kinds of misinformation: https://eavi.eu/ beyond-fake-news-10-types-misleading-info/
2. What's the big deal about fake news?
   - Ask students if they have seen fake news. Where did they see it? How did they know it was fake? 75 percent of us fall for fake headlines, and almost a quarter of adults have shared a made-up news story.
   - Ask students what might be consequences of believing fake news and sharing it? When people believe fake news, they are misinformed, and may make poor decisions. When people don't know what to believe, they may become frustrated, polarized, confused, fearful, distrustful, cynical and withdrawn. None of this helps society.
   - Watch C-SPAN's video on fake news consequences: www.c-span.org/ classroom/document/?6004. Ask students: "What consequences might impact you or your community?"
3. How is fake news created – and why?
   - Ask students who they think creates fake news. How easy do they think it is to create it?
   - Watch *Teaching Tolerance's* video. How does fake news become news? www. youtube.com/watch?v=qcRWkkSvfj0&feature=youtu.be Ask students: "How does this video change your opinion about fake news?"
   - Ask students: "Why do you think people create fake news?"
   - Watch "The business of fake news" video: https://video.vice.com/en_ us/embed/583cf8829b1abab240292954?ap=0&autoplay=0&autoStart=f alse&player_autoStart=false Ask students: "Do you think individuals who create fake news are responsible if people believe the fake news?" Why – or why not?
4. Why do we believe fake news?
   - Ask students: "Why do you think people believe fake news?"

- Share and discuss the article "News and America's kids": www. commonsensemedia.org/research/news-and-americas-kids
- Ask students: "What techniques do fake news use to get your attention?"
- Show www.aol.com. As you go through each story headline, ask students: "What images and words make you want to click on the story?" (ANSWERS: Words such as "shocking, unbelievable, best/worst"; images where the key element is missing). These techniques are called "clickbait."
- Watch how images can be edited: www.youtube.com/watch?v= x03bO2b30hY – and why. Ask students: "Have you ever seen similar image editing?" Ask them, "Now that you know how images can be edited, how does that impact how you look at fake news and other media messages?"

5. Become a fact-checker in four steps!
   - Look **through** (read through the entire website and links).
   - Look **up** (trace the source).
   - Look **across** (other sources).
   - Look **inside** (what are your own beliefs and biases?).
   - What looks like fake news?
     - 👁 Look THROUGH news
       - Share IFLA's infographic (www.ifla.org/publications/node/ 11174) about how to spot fake news.
       - Look at some examples of fake news websites (http://fakenewswatch. com/), and as a class pick out what makes them fake.
       - To see how much visuals impact a story, strip out all the visuals of a story, and then ask students to tell whether the story is true or fake.
     - 👁 Look THROUGH the news story
       - Walk through the CRAAP test (https://library.csuchico.edu/ help/source-or-information-good) with a couple of news stories.
       - Ask students to use the CRAAP test to examine a couple of news stories from the Credibility Challenge: www. annenbergclassroom.org/resource/the-credibility-challenge.
     - 👁 Look UP: Trace the news story
       - With the students, track the story:
       - Who wrote it? Use a search engine to find out more about the person or group. Are they on social media such as LinkedIn or Facebook?
       - Where did they get their information? Whom do they mention or cite? Did the story come from another site? Can you find the original news event?
       - Check the reliability of the location by using the WolframAlpha search engine (www.wolframalpha.com/) to check the weather in a certain place at a certain time to verify images or video.

- Trace the image by clicking the source code (and check the date/time of posting), comparing it to other pictures on a search engine, and use TinEye (https://tineye.com/) or Google Images to perform a reverse image search.
- Ask students in pairs to trace a current news story, and then compare their efforts with another pair.
- ◉ Look ACROSS other news stories
    - Share AllSides (www.allsides.com/unbiased-balanced-news), which rates media bias, and searches across the political spectrum to provide balanced news. Show a sample news story and its variations.
    - Either preview or ask students to identify a news story to see how AllSides addresses it.
    - Using the news story that students researched, ask them to use AllSides to compare other versions of the story. Ask them: "How similar or different are the versions in terms of content and presentation?"
- ◉ Look IN: What are your beliefs and biases?
    - People bring their own backgrounds and beliefs as they experience a news story. Ask students: "When is a time that you didn't believe a story that you heard, saw or read? Why didn't you believe it? How did you FEEL at the time?" If you feel angry about a story, that may be a signal that it is fake or at least biased.
    - We tend to believe news that agrees with our existing knowledge base or beliefs. This is confirmation bias. Ask students to name a time when they experienced this bias. To combat that, look at both sides of an idea.
    - We tend to ignore bad or negative news. This is called the ostrich effect. Ask students to name a time when they experienced this bias. Sometimes we just have to face the facts.
    - We sometimes expect a group to look or act a certain way without getting all the information. Ask students to name a time when they experienced this bias. This is stereotyping. To combat, ask yourself if everyone is like that, or is it a majority or even just one person?
    - We tend to look at winners and outliers, overlooking the majority, so we misjudge the probabilities. Ask students to name a time when they experienced this bias. This is called survivorship bias. To combat that, consider the likeliness of the outcome (e.g., how easy is it to become a movie star? How often do people experience homelessness?).
- Try your ability to identify fake news
    - Ask students to try identifying fake and true news at Factitious: http://factitious.augamestudio.com/#/

- Discuss in class what they learned about evaluating news.
- Ask students to create their own fake news from a real news story, and see if they can fool their classmates. Then discuss what made the news story believable or not.

6. What are good news sources?
   - Ask students: "What news sources do you think are credible? How do you choose what news sources to believe?"
   - Watch the TED Ed talk "How to choose your news": www.youtube. com/watch?v=q-Y-z6HmRgI&feature=youtu.be. Ask students: "How does the video inform your choices?"
   - You're on the way to becoming news literate: able to access, understand, evaluate and interpret news messages.
   - Use your local libraries – and work with their librarians.

7. How does format shape news?
   - **Media literacy is the ability to access, evaluate, interpret, create and respond to information that is developed by the mass media, including social media, done for profit/influence/power as its main objective**.
   - Share five key concepts of critical media analysis:
     - Media messages are constructed.
     - Media messages are produced within economic, social, political, historical and aesthetic contexts.
     - The interpretative meaning-making processes involved in message reception consist of an interaction between the reader, the text and the culture.
     - Media have unique "languages," characteristics which typify various forms, genres and symbol systems of communication.
     - Media representations play a role in people's understanding of social reality.
   - Each medium has its "grammar."
   - Start with **periodicals**. Ask students, "What are your newspaper habits? When do you read the newspaper? What is your favorite part of the newspaper – and why?"
     - What are the elements of a newspaper? (e.g., sections, headlines, articles, ads, images)
     - What kind of information is covered on the front page and in each section?
     - Where will you find facts – and opinions?
     - Who creates the articles?
     - The most important information is usually on the front page, or the upper right-hand side; what news is considered more important – and less important? Why?
     - Ask students, "How does a magazine differ from a newspaper?" (e.g., frequency, paper quality, table of contents, article arrangement and length, topic focus, coverage of news).

- The language of **radio**
  - Ask students, "What are your radio habits? When do you listen? Where do you listen? What is your favorite station – and why?"
  - What are the elements of radio? (e.g., programs and items/selections, music, talking, announcers/hosts, ads)
  - What kind of information is covered; does it depend on the station – why or why not?
  - Where will you find facts – and opinions?
  - Who creates the content?
  - Weekly schedule: how does the information vary by day and by time? How does that reflect its value?
  - How does the fact that it is just sound impact its content?
  - What kind of news do you get on the radio, if any? Why?
- The language of **television**
  - Ask students, "What are the characteristics of television?" Consider:
    - Audience (broad and narrow focus).
    - Kind of information, including news.
    - Weekly schedule: how does the information vary by day and by time? How does that reflect its value?
    - Who creates television content?
    - What elements are used to convey content (image, sound, movement)?
  - Ask students, "Based on the above criteria, how does film differ from television? Is it a major source of news?"
  - Watch this video explain the language of camera shots (www. youtube.com/watch?v=MfIanZimZR8) and other film "grammar." Ask students, "How does cinematography impact the news message?" In class or as homework, ask students to analyze television ads in terms of the visual language used.
- The language of the **Internet**
  - Ask students, "What are your Internet habits? When do you use the Internet? Where do you use it? Why do you use the Internet?"
  - What are the elements of the Internet? (e.g., browser, search engines, websites, apps, links, ads)
  - Who is the audience?
  - What kind of information is covered; how do you find it?
  - Who creates the content?
  - How does the content get conveyed (e.g., text, image, sound, movement)?
  - What kind of news do you get on the Internet, if any? Where do you go to get it?
- Compare media in terms of news
  - In pairs, ask students to complete a table comparing media (Table 7.2):

TABLE 7.2 Middle school media comparison

	Audience	News content (quantity, quality, topics)	News creators	Medium's language	Use of language to influence
Newspapers					
Magazines					
Radio					
Television					
Internet					

- Evaluate media outlets: www.allgeneralizationsarefalse.com/wp-content/uploads/2018/01/Media-Bias-Chart_Version-3.1_Watermark-min.jpg
8. Act!
   - Tell students: "Apply your news and media literacy! Use your voice to take action! The best way to combat fake news is to provide counter stories."
   - Ask students: "What is a piece of news or issue that is important to you – one that you want to convince others to believe?" Ask the class to share ideas.
   - Ask students in pairs to create a news item or media message. Make sure that they: (1) identify the audience; (2) determine an effective medium to use; (3) take advantage of the medium's language to make a convincing case.
9. Expanding the curriculum
   - If you as an educator – or educational site – want to expand this curriculum, here are some directions to take:
     - Media Spot: https://themediaspot.org/
     - The News Literacy Project: https://newslit.org/
     - Center for Media Literacy Educator Resources: www.medialit.org/educator-resources
     - Media Education Lab Media Literacy Education: https://mediaeducationlab.com/sites/mediaeducationlab.com/files/Field%20Guide%20to%20Media%20Literacy%20.pdf
     - Common Sense Media: www.commonsensemedia.org/
     - Media Redesign: https://docs.google.com/document/d/1OPghC4ra6QLhaHhW8QvPJRMKGEXT7KaZtG_7s5-UQrw/preview
     - UCLA Critical Media Literacy: https://guides.library.ucla.edu/educ466
   - Another way to expand the curriculum is to go into more depth on the literacies associated with fake news:
     - Media literacy.
     - Visual literacy.

- • Digital literacy, including digital citizenship.
- • Numeracy/data literacy.
- • Information literacy.
- • Integrating the curriculum
- • Fake news curriculum is probably most effective if integrating into the existing curricular structure, ideally spread across the subject domains and developed by the teaching faculty as a whole. Here are some starting suggestions for learning activities in the disciplines.
  - • Language arts: Analyze fake news, write fake news.
  - • Social studies: Examine historical primary source collections (e.g., American Memory: www.loc.gov/collections/) to find examples of fake news; discuss how these documents impacted events.
  - • Mathematics: Locate and analyze misleading statistics, especially in graph format (e.g., Statistics How To (www.statisticshowto.com/misleading-graphs/) and in current news).
  - • Science: Compare news perspectives about controversial science (e.g., climate change, cloning).
  - • Arts: Analyze advertisements and propaganda for fake news (e.g., Mind over Media: https://propaganda.mediaeducationlab.com/).
  - • Health and P.E: Locate and analyze fake news/claims about health and fitness (e.g., The Health Wrap: https://croakey.org/the-health-wrap-flu-shot-fake-news-assisted-dying-and-the-us-opioid-crisis/).

The bottom line? "An enlightened citizenry is indispensable for the proper functioning of a republic. Self-government is not possible unless the citizens are educated sufficiently to enable them to exercise oversight. It is therefore imperative that the nation see to it that a suitable education be provided for all its citizens." Thomas Jefferson

Fake news: A high school curriculum

Fake News Units

1. What is fake news, and why does it matter?
2. What is the fake news communication cycle?
3. What are strategies for identifying fake news?
4. What is the role of media literacy relative to fake news?
5. How can fake news be addressed?
6. Extending the fake news curriculum

1. What is fake news, and why does it matter?
   a. Defining fake news
      • Ask learners to share their perceptions of fake news. They can make a concept map about fake news. Share their perceptions.

- Define fake news: "Fake news is deliberate, published disinformation/hoax/lie purported to be real news."
- Compare fake news with other kinds of misinformation: https://eavi.eu/beyond-fake-news-10-types-misleading-info/. Ask the class to brainstorm some possible examples, or divide the class into ten small groups to locate examples of each online.

b. What's the big deal about fake news?
- Ask students if they have seen fake news. Where did they see it? How did they know it was fake? Share the status of fake news.
- 75 percent of us fall for fake headlines, and almost a quarter of adults have shared a made-up news story.
- During the latter part of the 2016 Presidential campaign, fake news was shared and commented more than real news.
- Ask the same small groups to explore this statistics portal, which shows statistics and facts about fake news: www.statista.com/topics/3251/fake-news/. Then have them report out, and postulate about the possible consequences of these facts.

c. What are the consequences of fake news?
- Ask students what might be consequences of believing fake news and sharing it? When people believe fake news, they are misinformed, and may make poor decisions. When people don't know what to believe, they may become frustrated, polarized, confused, fearful, distrustful, cynical and withdrawn. None of this helps society.
- C-SPAN shows fake news sites and effects on democracy: www.c-span.org/classroom/document/?6004. Then show Radiolab's video on the future of fake news: http://futureoffakenews.com/. Ask students: "How do these videos alter your opinion about fake news?"

d. Is fake news new?
- Ask students if they think that fake news is new?
- The term is new but the concept is old. With language comes truth and lies. News, then, reflects both possibilities. With each "new" mass media format – be it the printing press, radio, television or the Internet – has come fake news.
- Ask students to examine hoaxes throughout history (http://hoaxes.org/archive/display/category/history), with each group analyzing one historical period in light of fake news; ask them how these hoaxes compare with fake news – and why.
- The article about 19th century fake news reporting (https://theconversation.com/techniques-of-19th-century-fake-news-reporter-teach-us-why-we-fall-for-it-today-75583) asks the question: "How much do you truly know first-hand, from personal experience, compared to what you know from schoolbooks, television, newspapers and the Web?" Have the students answer the question in class, and then read the article as homework. Ask them to give a

couple of examples of current fake news that reflects the 19th century fake news practice.

2. What is the fake news communication cycle?

- Ask students: "Guess how much data is generated in one minute?" Then show the infographic: www.socialmediatoday.com/news/how-much-data-is-generated-every-minute-infographic-1/525692/

- Fake news follows an communication cycle – as does all other information.

   a. How is fake news created – and why?

      - Ask students: "Who do you think creates fake news? How easy do you think it is to create it?"

      - Ask students: "Why do you think people create fake news?" Ask them to watch "The business of fake news" video: https://video.vice.com/en_us/embed/583cf8829b1abab240292954?ap=0&autoplay=0&autoStart=false&player_autoStart=false. Ask students: "Do you think individuals who create fake news are responsible if people believe the fake news?" Why – or why not?

      - Watch the TED Ed video "How false news can spread": www.youtube.com/watch?v=cSKGa_7XJkg&feature=youtu.be. Ask students, "How easy would it be for you to create and get your news disseminated?"

      - Ask students, "How do you access news? How do you choose what to access? Do any barriers impact what and how you access news?"

   b. How do we perceive news?

      - Share and discuss the article Horrigan, J. (2017). *How people approach facts and information*. Washington, DC: Pew Research Center. (www.pewresearch.org/internet/2017/09/11/how-people-approach-facts-and-information/). Ask students: "Which group best represents you?"

      - Ask students to read Pew Research Center's report "The modern news consumer": www.journalism.org/2016/07/07/the-modern-news-consumer/. Ask students: "Does this report align with your own experience? How does it impact access to fake news?"

      - Ask students: "What techniques does news use to get your attention?"

      - Show www.aol.com. As you go through each story headline, ask students: "What images and words make you want to click on the story?" (ANSWERS: Words such as "shocking, unbelievable, best/worst"; images where the key element is missing). These techniques are called "clickbait."

      - Watch how images can be edited: www.youtube.com/watch?v=x03bO2b30hY – and why. Ask students: "Have you ever seen similar image editing?" Ask them, "Now that you know how images can be edited, how does that impact how you look at fake news and other media messages?"

- Share this visualization of trust levels of news sources by ideological group: www.journalism.org/2014/10/21/political-polarization-media-habits/pj_2014-10-21_media-polarization-01/. Ask students: "What patterns in fake news might you make relative to the data captured in this visualization?"

c. Why do we believe in fake news?
- Ask students, "Why do you think we believe in fake news?"
- Have the class watch the PBS video "Facts don't win fights": www.youtube.com/watch?v=kyioZODhKbE
- Share the infographic "Cognitive bias survival guide": www.geekwrapped.com/cognitive-bias-survival-guide. Ask students to self-identify some of the biases that they have exhibited. Ask them to identify one action they will take to overcome that bias.
- Ask students: "What can you do to read news more objectively?"

3. What are strategies for identifying fake news?
Become a fact-checker in four steps!
- Look **through** (read through the entire website and links).
- Look **up** (trace the source).
- Look **across** (other sources).
- Look **inside** (what are your own beliefs and biases?).
  a. What looks like fake news?
    - Ask students: "What looks like fake news?"
    - To see how much visuals impact a story, strip out all the visuals of a story, and then ask students to tell whether the story is true or fake.
    - Ask students to locate one real and one fake, and have them strip the layout. See if they can bluff their classmates in determining which news story is fake.
  b. ☉ Look THROUGH news.
    - Share IFLA's infographic about how to spot fake news: www.ifla.org/publications/node/11174.
    - Look at some examples of fake news websites (http://fakenewswatch.com/?so=1), and as a class pick out what makes them fake.
  c. ☉ Look THROUGH the news story.
    - Walk through the CRAAP test (https://library.csuchico.edu/help/source-or-information-good) with a couple of news stories.
    - Ask students to use the CRAAP test to examine a couple of news stories from the Credibility Challenge: www.annenbergclassroom.org/resource/the-credibility-challenge.
  d. ☉ Look UP: Trace the news story.
    - With the students, track the story:

- Who wrote it? Use a search engine to find out more about the person or group. Are they on social media such as LinkedIn or Facebook?
- Where did they get their information? Whom do they mention or cite? Did the story come from another site? Can you find the original news event?
- Check the reliability of the location by using the WolframAlpha search engine (www.wolframalpha.com/) to check the weather in a certain place at a certain time, to verify images or video.
- Trace the image by clicking the source code (and check the date/time of posting), comparing it to other pictures on a search engine, and use TinEye (https://tineye.com/) or Google Images to perform a reverse image search.
- Ask students in pairs to trace a current news story, and then compare their efforts with another pair.

e. ☞ Look ACROSS other news stories.
- Share AllSides (www.allsides.com/unbiased-balanced-news), which rates media bias, and searches across the political spectrum to provide balanced news. Show a sample news story and its variations.
- Either preview or ask students to identify a news story to see how AllSides addresses it.
- Using the news story that students researched, ask them to use AllSides to compare other versions of the story. Ask them: "How similar or different are the versions in terms of content and presentation?"

f. ☞ Look IN: What are your beliefs and biases?
- People bring their own backgrounds and beliefs as they experience a news story. Ask students: "When is a time that you didn't believe a story that you heard, saw or read? Why didn't you believe it? How did you FEEL at the time?" If you feel angry about a story, for instance, that may be a signal that it is fake or at least biased.
- Share the "Cognitive bias survival guide": www.geekwrapped. com/cognitive-bias-survival-guide. As homework, ask students to self-identify their biases, and to state why they will overcome their biases.

g. Try your ability to fact-check like a pro.
- Ask students to try identifying fake and true news at Factitious: http://factitious.augamestudio.com/#/.
- Discuss in class what they learned about evaluating news.
- Ask students to create their own fake news from a real news story, and see if they can fool their classmates. Then discuss what made the news story believable or not.

h. What are good news sources?

- Ask students: "What news sources do you think are credible? How do you choose what news sources to believe?"
- Watch the TED Ed talk "How to choose your news": www. youtube.com/watch?v=q-Y-z6HmRgI&feature=youtu.be. Ask students: "How does the video inform your choices?"
- Ask students to explore University of Texas Libraries' guide on finding news and news evaluation: http://guides.lib.utexas.edu/ news. Ask students to visit their school or public library, and identify which news sources they carry.
- Tell students: "You're on the way to becoming news literate: able to access, understand, evaluate and interpret news messages."

4. What is the role of media literacy relative to fake news? How does format shape news?

- **Media literacy is the ability to access, evaluate, interpret, create and respond to information that is developed by the mass media, including social media, done for profit/influence/power as its main objective**.
- Share the five key concepts of critical media analysis:
  - Media messages are constructed.
  - Media messages are produced within economic, social, political, historical and aesthetic contexts.
  - The interpretative meaning-making processes involved in message reception consist of an interaction between the reader, the text and the culture.
  - Media have unique "languages," characteristics which typify various forms, genres and symbol systems of communication.
  - Media representations play a role in people's understanding of social reality.
- Each medium has its "grammar"
  a. Start with **periodicals**. Ask students, "What are your **newspaper** habits? When do you read the newspaper? What is your favorite part of the newspaper – and why?"
     - What are the elements of a newspaper? (e.g., sections, headlines, articles, ads, images)
     - What kind of information is covered on the front page and in each section?
     - Where will you find facts – and opinions?
     - Who creates the articles?
     - The most important information is usually on the front page, or the upper right-hand side; what news is considered more important – and less important? Why?
     - Ask students, "How does a magazine differ from a newspaper?" (e.g., frequency, paper quality, table of contents, article arrangement and length, topic focus, coverage of news).

b. The language of **radio**
    - Ask students, "What are your radio habits? When do you listen? Where do you listen? What is your favorite station – and why?"
    - What are the elements of radio? (e.g., programs and items/ selections, music, talking, announcers/hosts, ads)
    - What kind of information is covered; does it depend on the station – why or why not?
    - Where will you find facts – and opinions?
    - Who creates the content?
    - Weekly schedule: how does the information vary by day and by time? How does that reflect its value?
    - How does the fact that it is just sound impact its content?
    - What kind of news do you get on the radio, if any? Why?

c. The language of **television**
    - Ask students, "What are the characteristics of television?" Consider:
        - Audience (broad and narrow focus).
        - Kind of information, including news.
        - Weekly schedule: how does the information vary by day and by time? How does that reflect its value?
        - Who creates television content?
        - What elements are used to convey content (image, sound, movement)?
    - Ask students, "Based on the above criteria, how does film differ from television? Is it a major source of news?"
    - Watch this video explain the language of camera shots and other film "grammar": www.youtube.com/watch?v=MfIanZimZR8. Ask students, "How does cinematography impact the news message?"
    - In class or as homework, ask students to analyze television ads in terms of the visual language used.

d. The language of the **Internet**
    - Ask students, "What are your Internet habits? When do you use the Internet? Where do you use it? Why do you use the Internet?"
    - What are the elements of the Internet? (e.g., browser, search engines, websites, apps, links, ads)
    - Who is the audience?
    - What kind of information is covered; how do you find it?
    - Who creates the content?
    - How does the content get conveyed? (e.g., text, image, sound, movement)
    - What kind of news do you get on the Internet, if any? Where do you go to get it?

TABLE 7.3 High school media comparison

	Audience	News content (quantity, quality, topics)	News creators	Medium's language	Use of language to influence
Newspapers					
Magazines					
Radio					
Television					
Internet					

  e. Compare media in terms of news
    • In pairs, ask students to complete a table comparing media (Table 7.3):
5. How can fake news be addressed? Act!
 • Tell students: "Apply your news and media literacy! Use your voice to take action! The best way to combat fake news is to provide counter stories."
 • Ask students: "What is a piece of news or issue that is important to you – one that you want to convince others to believe?" Ask the class to share ideas.
 • Ask students in pairs to create a news item or media message. Make sure that they: (1) identify the audience; (2) determine an effective medium to use; (3) take advantage of the medium's language to make a convincing case.
 • Ask students to explore the role of citizen journalists at https://edtechmagazine. com/k12/article/2011/11/transforming-students-citizen-journalists.
6. Expanding the curriculum
 • If you as an educator – or educational site – want to expand this curriculum, here are some directions to take:
  • Media Spot: https://themediaspot.org/
  • The News Literacy Project: https://newslit.org/
  • Center for Media Literacy Educator Resources: www.medialit.org/ educator-resources
  • Media Education Lab Media Literacy Education: https:// mediaeducationlab.com/sites/mediaeducationlab.com/files/ Field%20Guide%20to%20Media%20Literacy%20.pdf
  • Common Sense Media: www.commonsensemedia.org/
  • Media Redesign: https://docs.google.com/document/d/ 1OPghC4ra6QLhaHhW8QvPJRMKGEXT7KaZtG_7s5-UQrw/ preview
  • UCLA Critical Media Literacy: https://guides.library.ucla.edu/ educ466
 • Another way to expand the curriculum is to go into more depth on the literacies associated with fake news:

- • Media literacy.
- • Visual literacy.
- • Digital literacy, including digital citizenship.
- • Numeracy/data literacy.
- • Information literacy.
- • Integrating the curriculum
- • Fake news curriculum is probably most effective if integrating into the existing curricular structure, ideally spread across the subject domains and developed by the teaching faculty as a whole. Here are some starting suggestions for learning activities in the disciplines.
  - • Language arts: Analyze fake news, write fake news.
  - • Social studies: Examine historical primary source collections (e.g., American Memory: www.loc.gov/collections/) to find examples of fake news; discuss how these documents impacted events.
  - • Mathematics: Locate and analyze misleading statistics, especially in graph format (e.g., Statistics How To: www.statisticshowto.com/misleading-graphs/ and in current news).
  - • Science: Compare news perspectives about controversial science (e.g., climate change, cloning).
  - • Arts: Analyze advertisements and propaganda for fake news (e.g., Mind over Media: https://propaganda.mediaeducationlab.com/).
  - • Health and P.E: Locate and analyze fake news/claims about health and fitness (e.g., The Health Wrap: https://croakey.org/the-health-wrap-flu-shot-fake-news-assisted-dying-and-the-us-opioid-crisis).
  - • College/career readiness: Explore news-related careers.
  - • The bottom line? "An enlightened citizenry is indispensable for the proper functioning of a republic. Self-government is not possible unless the citizens are educated sufficiently to enable them to exercise oversight. It is therefore imperative that the nation see to it that a suitable education be provided for all its citizens." Thomas Jefferson

References

Agosto, D. (2018). *Information literacy and libraries in the age of fake news*. Santa Barbara, CA: Libraries Unlimited.

American Library Association. (2018). *Media literacy at your library: Learning and prototyping report*. Chicago, IL: American Library Association.

Debating Europe. (2020). Should media literacy be a compulsory school subject? www.debatingeurope.eu/2020/03/09/should-media-literacy-be-a-compulsory-school-subject/#.XpB7b1NKhp-

Friesem, Y. (2019). Teaching truth, lies, and accuracy in the digital age: Media literacy as project-based learning. *Journalism & Mass Communication Educator, 74*(2), 185–198.

Gingold, J. (2013). *Building an evidence-based practice of action civics*. Medford, MA: Tufts University.

Head, A., DeFrain, E., Fister, B., & MacMillan, M. (2019). Across the great divide: How today's college students engage with news. *First Monday, 24*(8), 1–18.

Huguet, A., Kavanagh, J., Baker, G., & Blumenthal, M. S. (2019). *Exploring media literacy education as a tool for mitigating truth decay*. Santa Monica, CA: RAND.

Jacobson, L. (2017). The smell test: In the era of fake news, librarians are our best hope. *School Library Journal, 63*(1), 24–29.

Potter, W. (2010). The state of media literacy. *Journal of Broadcasting & Electronic Media, 54*(4), 675–696.

INDEX

Printed in the United States
By Bookmasters